ORIGINAL
HARLEY-DAVIDSON
PANHEAD

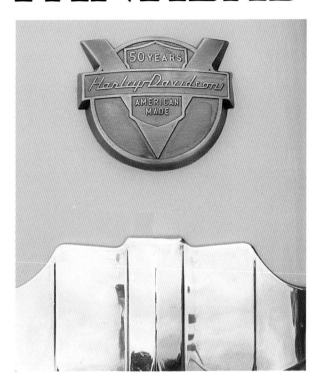

ORIGINAL
HARLEY-
DAVIDSON
PANHEAD

by Greg Field

First published in 2002 by MBI Publishing Company, Galtier Plaza, 380 Jackson Street, Suite 200, St. Paul, MN 55101-3885 USA

MBI Publishing Company books are also available at discounts in bulk quantity for industrial or sales-promotional use. For details write to Special Sales Manager at Motorbooks International Wholesalers & Distributors, Galtier Plaza, 380 Jackson Street, Suite 200, St. Paul, MN 55101-3885 USA

Library of Congress Cataloging-in-Publication Data Available

ISBN 0-7603-1062-9

Front cover: A 1961 Duo-Glide.

Frontispiece: This badge was fitted to the front fender of all Hydra-Glides for 1954.

Title page: A 1957 Hydra-Glide.

Contents page: The dash of a 1948 Panhead.

Back cover: A 1948 Panhead.

Edited by Chad Caruthers
Designed by Chris Fayers, Cardigan, Wales
Printed in China

Contents

Preface

Built for model years 1948 to 1965, the "Panhead" Hydra-Glides, Duo-Glides, and Electra Glides set the styles that are now Harley-Davidson. When Harley was really in trouble and needed something "new" to pull its bacon out of the fire, the company resurrected the look of the motor and the look of those machines, and that look was enthusiastically accepted once again on Harley's best-selling models, from the Softails to the Road King. Furthermore, the Panhead era was the last in which Harley-Davidson made sincere efforts to keep abreast of the latest in motorcycle technology. Combined, those things make the Panhead and its era among the most interesting in Harley history.

This book concentrates solely on the motorcycles and is not a history. I wanted to include as much detail as possible on the Panheads. Wherever possible, I tried to establish what is "correct" and "original" in the way of part finish, equipment finish, and in accessories for each year. However, this is not a discussion of the correct finish on every nut, bolt, and washer for every year of Panhead. For those who need such information, I heartily recommend Bruce Palmer's excellent book *How To Restore Your Harley-Davidson Motorcycle,* also published by Motorbooks International.

In my quest to establish what is original and correct, I used hundreds of sources, from original H-D order blanks, parts books, issues of *The Enthusiast,* sales literature, dealer bulletins, brochures, and advertisements, as well as magazine tests and numerous books. Where these sources contradicted one another or were vague, I tried to find the answer by talking to other riders and restorers and by looking at unrestored machines. However, it is always possible that some details may have eluded me, and I would be grateful for any errors that were pointed out to me.

Without question, the task of definitively establishing what is original and correct for all examples of even a single year of Panhead is probably not possible. These bikes were hand-assembled from whatever parts happened to be in the bin at the time, not necessarily with the parts the production engineers intended them to be fitted with. In stark contrast to the "just-in-time" inventory system the Harley-Davidson factory uses today, "inventory control" in the H-D factory during the Panhead era meant little more than refilling the parts bin sometime before or shortly after the last part was used. Thus, parts from new batches or even from new subcontractors were sometimes stacked in atop the older parts, resulting in some puzzling combinations of newer and older parts on some machines.

Thus, it's probably not possible to document every change or configuration that was ever built on every individual Panhead. Instead, I outline what I call the *nominal* configuration for each year of Panhead. What I mean by nominal is how most machines built during that year were equipped—how the documentation and weight of evidence suggests that Harley-Davidson intended them to be.

I also tried to make note of the many changes made during the production run for each year. Rather than allow myself to be driven crazy by trying to nail down the exact date or engine number on which each running change was implemented, I merely note that these changes took place early, in the middle of, or toward the end of the production run. In some cases, *Shop Dopes* or other Harley-Davidson documents list the engine number at which the change occurred and any out-of-sequence engine numbers that were fitted with the older parts. Wherever this information exists, I have included it in the text.

Another goal was to make sense of which models were available for each year and how many of each were built. These model and production-figures lists were published in Harley's 1993 book, *The Legend Begins,* and are often criticized for being inaccurate and misleading. The figures in *Legend*—compiled by a Harley employee in 1978—are the best available, but even Harley admits that there are apparent duplications in the figures, especially in those for wartime production, that may make them less than accurate. All model and production figures quoted in this book are from *Legend,* and are meant to be used for comparison only—not for authoritatively establishing which bikes are the most rare. Where they are most suspect, I have put forth my interpretation of the numbers.

Last, I tried to establish the correct paint colors that were available for each year. My lists sometimes differ from those published in other sources, so I think it is worth explaining why. Mine were compiled from H-D order blanks and from lists in *The Enthusiast* and include only those hues offered on the *Panheads.* It is certainly possible that some other colors were briefly offered for the Big Twins on certain order blanks and that discontinued or nonstandard colors were sometimes applied to individual bikes, but I could find no official documentation to prove this. As a result, I listed only those colors that are easily documented. If an owner restores a bike with a nonstandard color and intends to show it in an Antique Motorcycle Club of America (AMCA) event, he or she should be prepared to prove that the color was available on a new Panhead of that year.

An important caveat here: Throughout this book, I define "original" and "correct" as what was available from the factory *on a new machine*. To me, this includes only those items that were standard on new machines, were part of one of the available option groups, or were listed as options on the order blanks. A caveat to my caveat: I fully realize that what was available through the order blanks was prone to change during the production year (sometimes new items were handwritten on individual order blanks) and that sometimes the order blanks were incorrect, so this definition is something of a moving target.

I think it is okay to add period accessories to an otherwise correct machine, but I don't think it is okay to add accessories that were available in that year's accessory catalog if they differ in style from those Harley-Davidson intended for their new machines of that year. I know that my definition differs from the AMCA's definition, which allows accessories—Harley-Davidson and aftermarket—if the owner can prove they were available that year.

Why did I choose a different definition? Because I think the AMCA's definition works in most cases, but when interpreted literally it leads to some puzzling contradictions. Many Harley-Davidson parts and accessories were still listed in the accessory catalogs long after they were superseded by new-style parts on new machines. One of many examples of this is the fender tips used on 1959 and later Panheads. The older, bombardier-style front (correct for later 1948 and 1949 springer Panheads) and rear (correct for later 1948 through 1958 Panheads) are available through the 1960 accessory catalog. Does this mean these older-style parts are correct for newer machines? In my opinion, no. If the type of part in question (fender tip, bumper, or whatever) was available on a new machine, I define as correct only the specific style of part that would have been fitted by

the factory to a new machine. Also, Harley's parts catalogs list newer parts as being applicable to older machines. Does this mean the newer parts are correct for the older machines? Again, I say the answer is no.

If an owner wishes to restore his or her machine with the intent of having it judged at an AMCA event, it would be wise to restore it to the most easily documented form—the nominal form—so that the judge will quickly recognize that all is correct and you both go home happy. If a restored bike differs even slightly from the nominal, the burden of proof that the bike is correct falls on the owner's shoulders, and the owner needs to have handy some documentation to prove that the feature in dispute is correct. To make it even easier to document, the restorer could pick one of the option groups Harley offered and restore the bike to include all those parts. By making my definition of "correct" even more restrictive than the AMCA's, I think I trod a safer path, for the reader and for myself. After all, I will not be there when your restored bike faces the judge.

My emphasis throughout this book is on originality. For the photographs, I tried to find unrestored or exactingly restored motorcycles whenever possible. Unfortunately, such bikes are very rare, so to show at least one example of some years' Panheads, it was necessary to show bikes that are restored to a different standard than the AMCA uses. One pair of bikes shown was restored to what their owner terms the "How Harley would do it today" standard, meaning that many parts that were Parkerized or cadmium-plated on stock machines were chrome-plated in restoration. Some owners paint many parts black rather than sending them off to be Parkerized. The owners of these bikes intended them to be daily riders, not showpieces, so practical considerations took precedence over originality. In the captions for the photographs, I often comment on what parts and finishes are correct or incorrect. These comments are not meant as criticisms of the owners, restorers, or bikes. Rather, they are intended to guide and inform the reader, and I hope the owners of the bikes shown will take no offense.

Acknowledgments

This book was such a huge effort, and I have many people to thank. If I have forgotten anyone, I hope my oversight will be forgiven.

For going way beyond the call and supplying help and assistance, without which this book would not have been impossible: Rob Carlson, Gary Strom, and Elmer Ehnes, of Kokesh Motorcycles in Spring Lake Park, Minnesota; Norm Gerlich and John Viljoen, of Antique Cycle Northwest in Seattle; and Scott Lange.

For sharing information, letting me photograph their Panheads, or helping me to locate bikes to shoot: Bob Bowes, George Breitung, John Burgin, and Steve White, of Vintage Motorcycles Northwest in Spanaway, Washington; the late, great Dave DeMartini, of Northwest Custom Cycle in Snoqualmie, Washington; Robin Gauthier of Southside Cycle in Nanaimo, British Columbia; Allan Girdler, Jody Heintzman, John and Judy McGuire, of Rochester Harley-Davidson in Rochester, Minnesota; Dave Monahan, Gary Nelson, Dan Olberg, Jerry Richards, Dr. Martin Jack Rosenblum, of the Harley-Davidson Motor Company; and Eugene Schrier.

For long-term encouragement and support: My parents, Laurie and Larry; my brothers and sisters, Scot, Shawn, Dawn, and Heather; and my good friends Owen Herman, Tom Samuelsen, and Joe Sova

For putting me up and putting up with me while in Milwaukee: Ray, Carol, Annie, Becky, Katie, Tracy, and Vicky Karshna; Ed and Jean Kwiecinski; Jeff and Jackie Ciardo; and Annie and Heidi Golombiewski.

Finally, to Jeni, who put up with so much obsessive behavior and gave up so much so that I had time to finish this manuscript.

Chapter 1
The 1948 Panheads

When Harley's revised overhead-valve twin made its debut for 1948, it was a slim, low-slung machine that differed little from the 1947 Knucklehead that it replaced. This machine was restored by Elmer Ehnes.

On the heels of World War II, having suffered the loss of thousands of American soldiers, the United States in the fall of 1945 was a country poised and ready to move on to better days. A boundless jubilation that glowed with the pride of war victory, fueled by the mass return of some of this country's greatest heroes, was beginning to emerge among the American people. The country was reinvigorated and ready to reinvent itself.

From the Harley-Davidson board room, the sunrise of the postwar era looked glorious. Spurred on by the Army, the company had revitalized and

retooled itself to build close to 100,000 copies of "the motorcycle that won the war." In the meantime, Harley-Davidson's engineering staff created new designs that took advantage of many of the lessons it learned during the war. Those designs still needed a few years of refining before they'd be ready for market, but in the meantime, Harley-Davidson was poised to crank out Knuckleheads in unprecedented numbers.

The market for Harley's big overhead-valve Knuckle looked as limitless as the Lake Michigan horizon stretching eastward of Milwaukee.

The most visible change to the revised overhead-valve twin was the chrome-plated rocker covers that eventually resulted in the nickname "Panhead." The yellow shown was not a standard color for 1948.

Millions of servicemen—including thousands of former Harley-mounted dispatch riders—were suddenly discharged, their wallets fat with money they couldn't spend at the front and their sense of adventure honed keen by war. On the home front, after years of sacrifice, gas rationing, reduced speed limits, and tire shortages, gearheads couldn't wait to cash in their war bonds and drive, drive, drive in rapid pursuit of the good life.

Unfortunately, that post-war sunrise was quickly obscured for Harley-Davidson Motor Company. New clouds of war rolled in from the east as the Soviet Union tightened its stranglehold on Eastern Europe and Mao's Communist forces marched toward victory in China. The terms "iron curtain" and "cold war" gained everyday usage, and Harley-Davidson was once again called on to sacrifice.

From any view that hides the rocker covers, it's tough to tell what changed to make the new machine, as shown on this unrestored 1948 FL.

The U.S. government's first volley in the cold war was the Marshall Plan. Implemented to contain the Soviets by rebuilding the war-ravaged economies of Europe and England, the Marshall Plan sent hundreds of millions of dollars in scarce raw materials such as steel and chromium overseas to America's economic competitors. At the same time, the plan drastically lowered import duties so that those competitors could then ship back the goods and undercut U.S. manufacturers, including Harley-Davidson. While the Marshall Plan

may have contained communism abroad, it was a one-two punch that really hindered capitalism at home, and for certain in Milwaukee.

As a result of getting only a fraction of the steel, chromium, aluminum, and rubber it needed, Harley-Davidson couldn't build enough Knuckleheads in 1946 and 1947 to meet the demand. Waiting lists for new Harleys didn't begin in the 1990s. Guys who wanted a new Harley in the late 1940s often had to wait. Those who didn't want to wait looked to the other motorcycle makers.

Only one group of makers had a seemingly limitless supply of new bikes to offer: the British. While the U.S. government was reining in Harley-Davidson, the British government put the spurs to its motorcycle industry by forcing it to export 75 percent of its output or face reduced quotas of the same scarce materials Harley was being denied.

Only the United States had the cash to buy all those Brit bikes, and because of the reduced tariffs that were part of the Marshall Plan, those machines were artificially cheap. They were also light, fast, and fun, and there weren't enough Harleys to go around. Instead of the trickle of Triumphs and Nortons that had been imported before the war, 1946 brought a flood. England exported nearly 10,000 motorcycles to the United States in 1946 and more than another 15,000 in 1947.

Imagine the frustration in Milwaukee. After barely surviving the Great Depression and helping win the war, you're bitten by governmental policy—right as you venture into a time that should be one of limitless opportunity! Did the company pout, cry foul, or scream, "That's not fair?" Nope. Those tactics would come later, but for now, Harley chose to compete.

The company and its engineers didn't immediately counter the British threat with similar machines. That, too, came later, with the launch of the K-models and Sportsters. Rather, in the late 1940s, Harley-Davidson conceded the performance market to the British manufacturers and steered its overhead big twin line down a new road, one that led not to lighter weight nor greater performance, but to greater civility and refinement—and success.

That more-refined Harley made its debut in the fall of 1947, in time for the 1948 model year. At first glance, the 61- and 74-valve overhead engines didn't look very new. In fact, nothing was really new, except the whole top end of the engine. But what a difference a new top end can make, with aluminum cylinder heads for cooler running and hydraulic valve lifters to reduce engine noise and maintenance.

Most noticeable from the outside of the engines were the curious new valve covers that looked like chrome-plated cake pans atop each cylinder head. Though Harley didn't even have a

name for the new model, Harley enthusiasts soon began referring to it as the "Panhead," and a new legend and era began.

Models, Prices, and Option Groups

Like the last of the Knuckleheads, the first-year Panheads were available in two displacements: 61 cubic inches (1,000cc) for the E models and 74 cubic inches (1,200cc) for the F models.

Order blanks listed three versions of each: the 48E (61 cubic inches with 6.5:1 compression ratio), 48EL Special Sport Solo (61-cubic-inch engine with 7:1 compression), 48ES (61 cubic inches with 6.5:1 compression ratio and sidecar gearing), 48F (74 cubic inches with 6.6:1 compression ratio), 48FL Special Sport Solo (74 cubic inches with 7:1 compression ratio), and 48FS (74 cubic inches with 6.6:1 compression and sidecar gearing). Order blanks also list a special "police combination" of the three-speed transmission and medium gearing.

A note on engine serial numbers. The serial number prefix stamped on the left engine case at the Harley factory specified the year and model of engine, but not the extras, such as sidecar gearing for 1948 or hand or foot shifts for later years. Thus,

a 1948 FL motor would show a serial number "48FLxxxx." Similarly, a 1948 F motor would show a serial number of "48Fxxxx," and a 1948 FS sidecar twin would also show a serial number of 48Fxxxx, not 48FSxxxx.

The 61models listed for $635, and the 74models listed for $650. The four-speed transmission was standard, but the optional three-speed and three-speed with reverse were available at no extra cost. Per usual Harley-Davidson practice, however, these prices were misleading, because all new 1948 Panheads had to be ordered with one of three solo option groups, one sidecar group, or one police group, which added to the cost.

The Deluxe Solo Group sold for $92 and consisted of the following items: steering damper, front safety guard, jiffy stand, 5.00x16-inch tires, hydraulic shock absorber, colored shifter knob, deluxe solo saddle, deluxe saddlebags, rear safety guard, chrome air cleaner, chrome headlamp, chrome fender tips, chrome exhaust-pipe covers, chrome rims, chrome front-fender lamp, chrome tail lamp, chrome generator end cover, chrome relay cover, chrome timer cover, chrome foot-lever-bearing cover, chrome chain-inspection plate, and chrome clutch cover.

Early-1948 Pans were fitted with black-painted cylinders and exhaust pipes (as shown on this unrestored machine), but later machines were fitted with silver-painted cylinders and exhaust pipes.

This bike displays the correct outer primary cover for 1948 and 1949 Panheads. Note that the screws holding the chain-inspection cover—the small, round cover in the middle of the "diamond"—are at three o'clock and nine o'clock; on 1951–1954 covers, the screws are at six o'clock and twelve o'clock. The outer primary covers were all painted black from the factory, but chrome covers for the chain-inspection cover and clutch cover were optional.

The Sport Solo Group sold for $59.25 and included a steering damper, front safety guard, jiffy stand, 5.00x16-inch tires, hydraulic shock absorber, colored shifter knob, deluxe solo saddle, chrome air cleaner, chrome headlamp, chrome fender tips, chrome exhaust-pipe covers, chrome front fender lamp, chrome rims, chrome tail lamp, chrome generator end cover, chrome relay cover, chrome timer cover, and chrome foot-lever-bearing cover.

The Utility Solo Group sold for $24 and included the following items: steering damper, front safety guard, jiffy stand, 5.00x16-inch tires, chrome front-fender lamp, and chrome air cleaner.

The Utility Group for Sidecar Motorcycles sold for $35.50 and included steering damper, front safety guard, 5.00x16-inch tires, hydraulic shock absorber, chrome fender lamp, and chrome air cleaner.

The Standard Police Group sold for $73 and included the following items: steering damper, front safety guard, jiffy stand, 5.00x16-inch tires, chrome front-fender lamp, chrome air cleaner, hydraulic shock absorber, rear-wheel siren, speedometer hand control, and deluxe solo saddle. In addition, departments could order a police plate in place of the fender lamp for no additional charge.

Many of the items in the option groups were available separately, as were many options not included in these groups. For more information on these options and their prices, see *The Legend Begins*, published by Harley-Davidson, Inc. in 1993.

Factory Paint Options

Four different colors were available for 1948 Panheads: Azure Blue, Flight Red, Brilliant Black, and Police Silver (Police Group only).

A bit of Panhead paint trivia: Paint on 1948 Harley-Davidson motorcycles was applied only after the parts were first "Bonderized" (a phosphate coating, similar to Parkerizing, that soaks up paint and bonds it to the metal, while also giving the metal an extra level of protection against corrosion).

The Panhead Motor

In overall specifications, the Panhead motor was identical to the Knucklehead motor it replaced: it was a 45-degree V-twin with a transverse "crankshaft" built up from flywheels and shafts; it used "knife-and-fork" connecting rods, two pushrod-operated overhead valves per cylinder, hemispherical combustion chambers and domed pistons, a single carb in the center of the V, pressure oiling, a single four-lobed camshaft, and single-point "wasted-spark" ignition.

Look more closely, however, and you would see that many, many things were changed to make Harley's latest OHV power plant more refined, more reliable, more powerful, and easier to maintain. The hydraulic lifter system, aluminum cylinder heads, and a new oiling system are the main updates that turned the Knucklehead into the Panhead.

Hydraulic Lifter System

Before the first Panhead was introduced, all OHV motorcycle engines had been built with mechanically actuated valves. The older Knucklehead motor employed pushrods to transfer thrust from the tappets (which ride the rotating camshaft's lobes) to the individual rockers that opened the valves. The whole system operates efficiently if the proper clearances are maintained between all these moving parts. But maintaining these clearances is difficult. The engine heats up as it is runs, so the parts expand. Also, valve-train components inevitably wear, so some means must be used to compensate, or the clearances will continue to increase until the motor will no longer run.

For the Knucklehead and previous engines, Harley's engineers had dealt with these problems by making the pushrods adjustable, by using materials with complementary expansion rates, and by specifying a compromise clearance for the cold engine that would still leave adequate clearance when the engine reached operating temperature.

For the Panhead engine, the Milwaukee engineers borrowed a better idea from their counterparts in Detroit: hydraulic lifters.

Hydraulic lifters are miniature hydraulic rams that fill with oil during operation and expand to just take up any changes in driveline lash. When properly designed, these lifters eliminate lash and noise from the valve train and compensate for expansion as the engine warms up, while simultaneously compensating for wear in the parts. More important for the reluctant wrench, they free the owner from adjusting valves, one of those messy chores that takes up valuable riding time. After initial adjustment at the factory, the lifters typically don't need adjustment again until the engine is reassembled after a major repair.

For the Panhead, the hydraulic lifters had two main components—the cylinder and the plunger— and the whole lifter assembly was attached to the top of the pushrod. When the engine was started, oil was forced through the rocker-arm assembly to the hollow tip of the lifter's plunger, past a check ball to a small oil reservoir underneath the plunger. The check ball prevented the oil from immediately

escaping, so the cylinder continued to fill with oil until all the lash was taken up or until the plunger topped out against the retaining ring at the top of the cylinder bore, whichever happened first. (In the latter case, valve lash was beyond the range that the hydraulic lifters could accommodate, so the pushrods would have to be adjusted to take up the difference.)

Each cylinder and plunger was a matched set manufactured with the proper clearance to allow the oil to escape out of the cylinder and past the plunger at what Harley-Davidson specified only as a "definite leakage rate." This leakage was minor, but it gave the added benefit of a minor shock-absorbing and damping effect in the valve train. Oil lost through leakage was constantly replenished from the oil supplied by the rocker arm.

It wasn't just the lifters atop the pushrods that were new for 1948. Nearly every component of the valve train was new for 1948 in order to adapt the valve train to work with the hydraulic lifters and to make it oil-tight. Camshafts, tappets, tappet blocks, pushrods, pushrod tubes, and rocker arms were new, too. We'll start from the bottom and work our way up.

These Deluxe saddlebags were available early in the 1948 year but were eventually replaced by the King Size bags.

Camshafts

The 1948 Panhead cam retained the familiar four-lobe configuration introduced on the 1936 Knucklehead, but the lobes were given revised profiles to work better with the hydraulic lifters. The cam for 74 motors had a lift of 1.334 inches and a lobe width of 1.10 inches. The cam for the 61 motors had a lift of 1.328 inches and a lobe width of 1.10 inches. (For comparison, the cam used on Knucklehead motors from 1936–1947 had a lift of 1.22 inches and a lobe width of 0.875 inches.)

The cam for the 61 motors was used through the 1952 season (after which the 61 motor was dropped); afterward, it was fitted to the 74's FLE Traffic Combination motors built from 1953 to 1956. The cam for the 74 motor was used for all standard FL motors from 1948 to 1969 and in the 1955 FLH, the first year of the FLH.

Tappets and Tappet Blocks

The tappet blocks on the top of the right crankcase were now cast of aluminum (rather than of iron) and were unpainted. Less noticeable, the new blocks lacked oil-scavenging holes because oil from the heads was no longer returned to the cases through the pushrod tubes. These aluminum tappet blocks were used on 1948–1952 Panheads.

Front and rear tappet blocks were not interchangeable. The number 9-483 was cast in relief on the bottom of the front block, and the number 9-482 was cast in relief on the bottom of the rear block. Four straight-slot cadmium-plated screws with countersunk star-lock washers secured each tappet block to the crankcase on all 1948 and 1949 Pan motors. All four tappets were identical, and each consisted of a roller at the bottom to bear on the camshaft, a cylindrical body, and an adjuster screw (with lock nut) that threaded into the tappet body to allow adjustment of the pushrod length.

Pushrods and Pushrod Tubes

The new pushrods were 7½ inches long (before the lifters were installed), and, as previously described, a hydraulic lifter attached to the top of each pushrod to complete the connection from tappet to

rocker arm. This style of tappets, pushrods, and adjuster screws continued in use through 1952.

As on the Knucklehead motor, a pair of telescoping chromed steel tubes covered the pushrods to seal out dirt and seal in oil. Both tubes were redesigned for 1948, however, to make adjustments easier and for better sealing. They worked well, too, with the result that the upper and lower pushrod tubes introduced on the first Panhead were still in use on the last Panhead seventeen years later. The cork seals eventually wear out and cause leaks, but the system seals reasonably well if the seals are periodically replaced.

Rocker Arms

The rocker arms in the heads were also completely redesigned. We'll discuss those changes in the section describing the aluminum heads, except to note here that the rockers were revised to deliver oil to the new hydraulic lifters through the hollow pushrod ball socket on each rocker arm.

Harley's Panhead wasn't the first engine with hydraulic lifters, but it was the first production motorcycle engine with them, a fact that Harley emphasized in all its ads. When operated at cruising speeds in moderate weather, the lifters usually

Most of the chassis parts from the Knucklehead were carried over to the 1948 Panhead, including forks, wheels, headlight, fenders, horn, and front-fender light.

This style of speedometer was introduced on the 1948 models.

The unrestored 1948 in the foreground was a deluxe model when it was first ordered; it has all the options of the top-of-the-line Deluxe Solo Group, plus some more. Note the Deluxe Buddy Seat, well-worn from many years of use. The yellow rosettes behind the nickel stars on the seat's skirt are a distinguishing feature of the 1948 Deluxe Buddy Seat. The individual handrails on each side of the seat were the only rails available for 1948 Buddy Seats. A few features on this bike are not stock.

worked as advertised, but they also could take awhile to stop ticking after engine start-up or even to stay ticking in normal operation if the weather was hot, the oil dirty or substandard, or the revs were kept low. The lifters on some machines operated consistently, whereas many others ticked steadily.

Aluminum Cylinder Heads

At the end of World War II, thousands of fighter and bomber aircraft were flown home to be melted down into light, shiny ingots of aluminum. Prices for aluminum plummeted, and Harley-Davidson saw an opportunity.

Cylinder heads on the Knuckleheads had been cast iron because it is tough, long-lasting, cheap, and easy to cast into motorcycle parts. Cast iron unfortunately is heavy and slow to transfer heat, too. That latter characteristic manifested itself in overheating (particularly the rear cylinder and head) when Knuckleheads were run hard for long periods of time or in very hot weather.

Aluminum, by comparison, sheds heat much more quickly than iron and is much lighter. Aluminum, however, was so expensive before World

War II that its use was largely limited to the aircraft industry, so most foundries had not developed techniques for casting it. Despite that, Harley had used it on the relatively simple heads of some of its flat-head models, but the material was too expensive and risky in the prewar world to use for the complex castings of the overheads.

Another beneficial by-product of the war effort was that foundries all over the country had been forced to learn the technology of casting aluminum to make parts for warplanes, which meant the metal was a less-risky experiment for Harley's heads. So when it began to appear that aluminum would be cheaper and more plentiful in postwar America, Harley took this risk and designed new OHV heads around the metal.

The new cylinder heads for 1948 were not only made of aluminum, they were a complete redesign. The most noticeable difference was that the Knucklehead's aluminum rocker boss and separate covers for exhaust and intake valve trains on each head were replaced by a single pan-shaped cover that enclosed the top of each head and eventually inspired the Panhead name. The new covers lent a simple, more modern, finished look to the new

This "eagle" tip for the front fender was optional on early-1948 Panheads.

heads—and they were far less leaky than the Knucklehead's covers.

For 1948 only, these rocker covers were made of chrome-plated steel (later covers were made of stainless steel or aluminum, depending on the year). Twelve cadmium-plated, round-head Phillips screws with lock washers clamped each cover to its cylinder head, and a gasket sealed the gap. In an effort to muffle valve train noise, a felt pad was glued to the inside top of each cover.

Most of the parts under the cover were also new, including the valves, steel valve guides, lower spring collars, and the rocker arms, which rotated inside split center-mounted bearings bolted to the heads, rather than the fixed rocker shafts as they had on the Knucklehead.

Panhead heads also included internal passageways to route in oil to lubricate the valve train and to return oil to the sump. These changes are described in the next section, Oiling System.

The new valve train worked well, except that some early Panheads experienced problems with sticky and noisy intake valves because the intake guides didn't get an adequate oil supply.

Supplying gas and air to the new heads were the same black-painted carburetors, Linkert M-35 (standard, with 1⅛-inch venturi) or M-75 (with 1³⁄₁₆-inch venturi, optional for the 74 models) that were used on the late Knuckleheads. Gas-air mixture from the carburetor was delivered to each head through a T-shaped manifold attached by

large plumber nuts, like those used on the last Knuckleheads. Unlike those of the Knucklehead, however, the manifold and nuts used on the Panhead were cadmium-plated steel instead of Parkerized cast iron.

Exhaust gases were routed out of the heads and into the exhaust headers through the cast-in exhaust nipples added for 1948. The matching exhaust headers for 1948 were swaged to a larger diameter at the top to fit over this nipple. Above the exhaust port, on a boss between the first and second cooling fins, was a plugged hole that appeared only on 1948 and 1949 head castings.

This front-fender tip was introduced during the 1948 model year.

Note the way the front down tubes of the frame bend out like a wishbone near where the front safety guard attaches. This new frame is nicknamed the wishbone frame and was fitted to all 1948 Panheads.

On the underside of each head casting, between the pushrod holes, was the number "119 48 FRONT" or "119 482 REAR," cast in relief. These front and rear cylinder-head castings are correct for 1948 and 1949 Panheads.

Oiling System

On the old Knucklehead, oil to the top end was routed out of the gear case through an external oil pipe that branched to carry oil to each head. That oil was then returned to the gear case through the pushrod tubes. This system worked well enough, but the external lines were somewhat unsightly and prone to leaks.

For the Panhead, Harley-Davidson wanted better. Also, the addition of the hydraulic lifters meant certain changes to the oiling system anyway, so while they were at it, Harley's engineers reworked the whole oiling system to reduce leaks and to make the engine less of a "plumber's nightmare."

They did it by routing the oil in and out of the heads through internal passages. On the new motor, oil was pumped to each head through an oil passage in each cylinder and through internal passages in each head casting to the rocker bearings and then to the rockers and lifters. Return oil dripped into a passage in each head and through an oil-return passage in each cylinder to the crankcase. Of course, the revised oiling system required changes to the cylinders, heads, and crankcases.

The main difference between the new and the old cylinders was the internal oil passages in the new cylinders, bored from the base-gasket surface at the bottom to the head-gasket surface on the top. The oil-feed passage was on the right, and the oil-return passage was on the left.

Some familiar features returned on the new cylinders, however, including the lip along the top of the barrel (it had always been there on 61-ci barrels but not on 74-ci barrels; now it was used on both) and four mounting holes in the base. The cylinders were still cast of iron and were painted black. Some time during the production run, though, Harley-Davidson began painting the cylinders silver, and all Panhead cylinders from that point on were painted silver. This cylinder design was used, unchanged, through the 1952 model year.

While there is some truth to the notion that the Panhead motor was just a Knucklehead motor with a new top end, four significant parts were changed in the 1948 Panhead lower end and gear case: the left and right crankcases, cam gear, and gear-case cover. All of these changes were made to accommodate the new oiling system rather than because something needed fixing.

For 1948, both the left and right crank cases were modified to serve as part of the oil-return system. Return oil from the front cylinder flowed from the cylinder passages through a new passage in the left case to the scavenge sump, from which the oil pump returned it to the tank. Return oil from the rear head flowed out of the internal passage on the left side of the rear cylinder and into a new drain channel milled into the left case's base-gasket surface. This channel routed oil from the left side of the left crankcase, around the back of the case, where it flowed through a similar channel milled into the right case's base-gasket surface and along the channel to a drain hole into the case.

The left case was also updated on the inner side to improve oiling of the sprocket-shaft bearing. A cast-in V-shape funneled the oil dripping down the inside of the case into an oil hole to lubricate the bearing. This left case had the number "112-481" cast in relief on the inside of the case, along with a casting-date plate. This style of left crankcase was used through the 1952 model year.

The right case was also modified to serve a new role in the oil-feed system to the cylinder heads for 1948. The new right crankcases route feed oil from the oil pump to a passage at the right side of each cylinder base, rather than to a boss on the gear cover for an external oil line. This case had the number "112-48" cast in relief on the inside and was used through the 1951 model year and partway into 1952 (Harley-Davidson literature says only that the case style changed at "about" engine number FL3529).

Because it was no longer part of the chain in routing oil to the cylinder heads, the oil-feed hole on the top edge of the gear case cover for 1948 was plugged with a screw. Later in the year, a revised gear cover was released, having a steel plug pressed into the oil hole. Still later 1948 motors were fitted with covers that were not drilled for the oil hole.

In all other ways, the 1948 gear covers were identical to those of the last Knuckleheads, meaning that they were die-cast aluminum and the outside surface displayed eight cooling ribs, the breather tunnel (the tubelike ridge that goes across the cover from lower left to upper right), and the pinion-bushing boss. This last style of gear cover was used from late 1948 through 1950. The gear cover was fastened by straight-slot screws for 1948 and 1949.

Additional Changes and Features

As on pre-1940 Knuckleheads, pistons for the 1948 Panhead were offered in high-compression (7:1 ratio) and medium-compression (6.5:1 for Model Es, or 6.6:1 for Model Fs). Compression rings on 61-ci pistons were narrowed in width to $\frac{3}{32}$ inch (from $\frac{1}{8}$ inch on the Knucklehead), but the oil-control ring was widened to $\frac{3}{16}$ inch (from $\frac{1}{8}$ inch). Early-1948 74-ci pistons had an oil-ring groove $\frac{1}{8}$-inch wide and were fitted with a conventional oil-control ring.

The exhaust system for the 1948 Panhead was basically the same as the Knucklehead's, except that

the header pipes were swaged at the top to fit over the exhaust-port nipple. A stainless-steel strap clamp fastened each header to its nipple. The system had four pipes—front header, S-pipe, Y-pipe, rear header—and a muffler. The muffler was the rocket-fin style that had been used since 1941.

Mufflers were painted high-temperature black for 1948. Pipes on early 1948 Panheads were also painted high-temperature black, but sometime during the production run, Harley-Davidson started painting the exhaust pipes silver. Photos in 1948 issues of *The Enthusiast*, along with inspection of several unrestored 1948 machines, suggest that the change to silver-painted cylinders and silver-painted exhaust pipes occurred at about the same time. Optional chrome-plated flex-pipe covers were available as part of the Deluxe Solo or Sport Solo groups or separately, but neither a chrome-plated

The rocker covers and air cleaner were made of chrome-plated steel for 1948, but both were made of stainless steel for 1949.

Dashes on stock machines were painted the same color as the gas tanks.

major components were upgraded to accompany the new motor.

Wishbone Frames

The 1948 frame was the first of the "wishbone" frames, so called because when viewed from the front, the down tubes of the frame bend outward and then back down, much like the shape of a wishbone. These tubes were not flattened or fitted with mounting blocks for a horn on the motor side for 1948, as they would be on later frames.

A bracket for the front safety guard was welded between the two down tubes just above the wishbone bends, and a new safety guard was introduced to mount to this bracket. The new guard consisted of two tubular guard loops connected in the center by a sleeve. This sleeve was flattened and two holes were drilled through it for the mounting bolts. Front safety guards were painted black for 1948 and 1949. This style of safety guard was used through 1950, and 1950 was the first year they were available in chrome finish on a new Panhead.

The frame was fitted with a new steering-head forging, and that was fitted with a steering-head tumbler lock on the right side and a boss for the steering-damper pin for the forthcoming Hydra-Glide steering damper.

The upper motor mount was also revised. The new mount curved forward, whereas the upper mount on the Knucklehead frame dropped straight down from the backbone tube.

The frame carried over many familiar features, including the toolbox strap welded between the upper and lower rear frame tubes. Though the wishbone frame would be used through mid-1954, the wishbone for 1948 was the only one without horn-mount blocks on the motor side of the down tubes.

Speedometer

Also fitted to the 1948 Panhead was a newly designed Stewart-Warner speedometer. The circular, recessed center panel was bluish gray and enclosed the odometer (forward of center) and trip meter (aft of center) and had hash marks at 2-mile-per-hour intervals (all equal length but thicker at the 10-mile-per-hour marks) painted on the outside edge. The odometer and trip-meter numerals were black for miles and red for tenths, both on white backgrounds. The speedometer's outer ring was greenish gray and provided the background for the numbers, which were painted (10 through 120) on the underside of the glass in cream-ivory paint, along with the Harley-Davidson bar and shield at the rear edge. The pointer was painted red, the glass was flat (glass was convex on previous speedometers), the bezel was chrome plated, and the case was cadmium plated. This speedometer was used through the 1952 season.

muffler nor a stainless-steel muffler cover was available on a new machine that year.

The Panhead Chassis

Updating the motor rather than the chassis had been a logical decision for Harley-Davidson. The final Knucklehead's chassis and suspension—tubular cradle frame with rigid rear end, sprung saddle, and offset springer fork—were not cutting-edge stuff, but they were certainly adequate for the average road conditions and riders of the day and, more important, were in line with the Panhead's more conservative contemporaries.

Gas tanks, fenders, forks, wheels, primary-chain covers, tool box, oil tank, transmission, taillight, and many other parts were carried over from the last Knucklehead. Even so, several

Terminal Box

The lighting and ignition wires led to a new terminal box behind the spark coil. The terminal ends were crimped on (they had been soldered) and insulated with Vinylite plastic tubing.

Problems and Fixes

As was usual on a new Harley model, 1948 Pans had a few problems. The most common of these was valve-train noise as a result of partially collapsed lifters.

The root problem was that the lifters were at the top of the pushrods, at the farthest reaches from the oil pump. Harley's first attempted fix was to change the initial adjustment specification for the lifters from ⅟₁₆ inch compressed to ³⁄₃₂ inch compressed. Unfortunately, this change did little to solve the problem.

What the lifters needed was more oil pressure, especially at low rpm. Harley's engineers tried to meet that need with a new version of the oil pump for 1948 that company literature claimed gave a 25-percent increase in oil flow. The pump did provide more oil, but not enough at low rpm because it was defeated by the oil-pump governor, which was a centrifugal bypass valve that bled oil to the gear case at low rpm. This was a feature that was added to Harley-Davidson oil pumps in 1941 expressly to prevent over-oiling at low revs. This oversight was fixed on the last 75 1948 Panheads, which were fitted with a revised pump that omitted the oil-pump governor. Harley-Davidson also issued *Shop Dope* No. 278 (October 14, 1948), which described the procedure for converting the oil pump and directed dealers to convert oil pumps on all 1948 models not yet sold.

In a few cases, problems with ticking lifters were caused by mechanical defects, not by an inadequate oil supply. Early- to mid-1948 engines, for example, sometimes were plagued with noisy lifters because of oil leaks in the metal plugs that sealed the ends of rocker-arm oil passages. These plugs had a tendency to work themselves loose over time, and loose plugs bled off oil pressure to the ball socket and lifter. Toward the end of the model year, a new rocker was introduced that was drilled from only the pushrod end, and a steel plug was driven into the hole, eliminating the problem. These revised rocker arms were used through 1950. The pushrod ball sockets were also known to leak and break, so a new ball-socket design was introduced in late 1948 to eliminate this problem, too.

Despite all these fixes, some early Panheads ticked away, while the majority operated well. The oil problem was finally fixed for good in 1953, when the hydraulic lifters were moved to a new location between the pushrods and the tappets.

This "eagle" tip for the rear fender was used at the start of 1948.

This tip for the rear fender was introduced during 1948 to match the new front tip.

Sticky Intake Valves

Though the new valve train worked well, some early Panheads experienced problems with sticky and noisy intake valves because the intake guides didn't get an adequate oil supply. The intake valves were on the "uphill" side of each head, so oil flowed quickly away from the guides to the low side of the head.

To hold more oil near the intake guides, an "oil dam" was designed into the heads of motor numbers higher than 48E3111 and 48F3125. Instructions on how to fix the problem on earlier motors were the subject of *Shop Dope* No. 269, dated March 15, 1948, which recommended that all early-1948 motors be fitted with a new dam kit, provided free of charge by the factory, whenever they exhibited signs of sticking valves or when the heads were removed for other work. (As we shall later see, the real fix for this problem was implemented in 1949 when an intake-valve oiler was added to the top shell of the intake bearings.)

Over-Oiling

The extra capacity of the new oil pump (designed to prevent starving of the valve lifters) sometimes burned too much oil because the extra oil overwhelmed the piston rings. The need for these rings was even greater once the oil-pump governor was omitted later in the year, as discussed already. From motor number 58FL10184 on, new pistons were fitted to the 74 models, and these pistons featured a ³⁄₁₆-inch oil-ring groove and a new "vented"

Harley's updated engine deserved updated suspension, and that's what Harley-Davidson gave it in the years that followed.

Deluxe Solo Group or could be ordered separate. This style of Deluxe Solo Seat is correct for 1947–1954 Big Twins.

The Deluxe Buddy Seat was a much larger seat, designed to hold both rider and passenger. It was covered in leather and had a plastic skirt decorated with nickel studs and nickel stars on yellow-plastic rosettes. This style of buddy seat was optional for 1947 and 1948.

Fender Tips, Safety Guards, Windshields, and Saddlebags

New, chrome fender tips were optional for 1948. Both front and rear tips had a winged design that looked like a World War II bombardier's wings stamped in relief in the center of each. The front fender tip was optional for 1948 and 1949 spring-fork models. The rear tip was optional through 1958.

A rear safety guard was one of the most popular options. The 1948 guard was the same guard that had been used since the 1930s. It was offered only in black-painted finish (chrome-plated guards were not offered until 1950). This guard was an option through 1957.

Perhaps the most popular option for a spring-fork Panhead was the Silver King handlebar-mounted sport windshield, which did an excellent job of protecting the rider from the wind.

Next most popular was probably the King-Size saddlebags. These are large, black leather bags decorated with orange plastic piping (the colored piping frames the top of the cover, the lower edge of the cover, and the lower edge of the side), three rows of nickel dots on top of the cover, a single row of nickel dots along the lower edge of the cover, another row of dots curving along the lower edge of the side, three "Western" buckles (wide and rounded at the top, tapering toward the bottom), four large silver teardrop pieces (arranged with the thick end forward), one teardrop ahead of the front buckle, one between the first and second buckles, one between the second and third buckles, and one behind the third buckle, three nickel dots arranged vertically below the middle two teardrops, and two nickel dots in a vertical row on the side of the cover and aligned with the buckle straps. The hanger is chrome plated and has four mounting holes. These bags are correct for 1948 and 1949 Panheads.

oil-control ring. Later 61-ci pistons were also fitted with the vented ¾₆-inch oil-control ring.

Options and Accessories

Wartime restrictions on the use of chrome, aluminum, and other "essential" materials resulted in very plain-looking motorcycles from 1942 to 1947. On these machines, parts that would normally have been chrome plated were painted white or black, and there were virtually no accessories available.

For 1948, fortunately, dozens of options were once again available to dress up a new Harley. We don't have room to list them all here, so we'll cover just the most popular items.

Seats

Two optional seats were offered, the Deluxe Solo and Deluxe Buddy seats. The solo seat had thicker foam padding than the Standard Solo seat. It was covered in leather, and had a three-piece skirt around the seat's rear. The skirt was decorated with a plastic rosette on each side, a row of nickel pieces in line with the rosettes, and a line of nickel dots along the skirt's lower edge. It was included in the

Production for 1948

By any measure, the first Panhead was a huge success. During the 1948 production run, 12,924 Panheads were built, and Harley-Davidson was still unable to meet demand. This total included 198 Model ES, 4,321 Model EL, 334 Model FS, and 8,071 Model FL. Again, the "S" in "ES" and "FS" was not stamped into the motor as part of the serial number.

Chapter 2

The 1949–1957 Hydra-Glides

With the new motor a proven success in 1948, Harley looked to the rest of the bike for 1949 and restyled the whole bike in a bold, modern (for its day) fashion that was as different from the old springer-forked bikes as the first Knucklehead was from the old flathead it replaced.

The most noticeable part of that look was the all-new front end, dominated by massive-looking telescopic forks. The new fork contributed more than looks, however. It also gave the Panhead a smoother ride and better handling.

"Hydra-Glide" was the name Harley-Davidson gave to its innovative new hydraulic forks, and they were available only on the Panheads that year. Before long, the Panheads themselves became known by the Hydra-Glide moniker, and Harley-Davidson began encouraging the trend by offering optional front-fender badges featuring the name.

Over time, the more modern look of the Hydra-Glide proved as timeless as that of the Knuckleheads and springer Panheads that preceded it. Prove it to yourself by comparing one to the Heritage Softail of today or one of the many imitations put out by Harley's Japanese competitors. In many ways, the Hydra-Glides were the classic Pans.

New hydraulically damped telescopic forks were the big change for 1949. Harley-Davidson named these forks "Hydra-Glide," and before long, the bikes themselves became known as "Hydra-Glides."

The tank-mounted shifter was no longer connected to a three speed transmission. In 1949, the standard transmission contained four forward gears. An optional sidecar transmission featured three forward and one reverse gear.

and F, making the ES and FS models. Per usual Harley-Davidson practice, however, only the "E" or the "F," not the "S," were stamped into the case as part of the serial number. All were fitted with Hydra-Glide forks as standard.

Spring forks were available by special order for sidecar-equipped motorcycles (although some 1949 springer Pans were probably ordered as solo models). All bikes so equipped were designated EP, ELP, FP, or FLP, depending on which motor was fitted. Sidecar gearing was also optional for both chassis, and bikes so fitted were designated ES, ELS, EPS, ELPS, FS, FLS, FPS, or FLPS, depending on which motor and front end was fitted. Though the "S" was not stamped on the motor as part of the serial number, the "P" sometimes was, but it was stamped at the end of the number (e.g., FL1234P, not FLP1234). Even though Harley-Davidson offered sidecar-equipped bikes with the Hydra-Glide forks, the company recommended that all sidecar and package-truck bikes be equipped with the spring forks because the Hydra-Glide had insufficient trail for good stability with a sidecar or package truck.

The three-speed transmission was no longer an option for 1949 and later bikes; the only option to the standard four-speed was the three-speed with reverse.

Base-model 61s carried a retail price of $735, and the 74s carried a retail price of $750. (Spring-fork model prices were not available.) These prices were for bare-bones models (without an air cleaner, side stand, or front safety guard) that were only meant for use as the base bike for sidecar or package-truck use. Also, per usual Harley-Davidson practice, these prices were misleading because all new 1949 Hydra-Glides were shipped with one of the three solo option groups, one sidecar group, or one police group, which added to the cost.

The Utility Solo Group was the cheapest option at $21.15 ($24.75 for springer models), thus the real base price for a stripper was a bit higher than Harley's figures indicate, and much higher if the rider ordered the usual touring accessories.

The Deluxe Solo Group sold for $115 and consisted of the following items:
- front safety guard
- jiffy stand
- 5.00×16-inch wheels and tires
- stainless-steel air cleaner, timer cover, generator end cover, primary-chain-inspection cover, clutch cover, fork trim, foot-lever-bearing cover, and muffler shield
- chrome relay cover, headlight, taillight, rear fender tip, exhaust-pipe covers, rims, hub caps, rear bumper, and front chrome parking lamps
- colored shift ball
- deluxe solo saddle
- pair of King Size saddlebags

The 1949 Hydra-Glides

The new front end was the biggest—but not the only—chapter in the Panhead story for 1949. Along with the new front end came a bigger front brake, new fenders, a revised frame, and many other changes.

Models, Prices, and Option Groups

The year 1949 saw two basic versions of the Hydra-Glide offered in each displacement size, the 61-ci models E and EL and the 74-ci models F and FL. In addition, sidecar gearing could be ordered on the E

- rear safety guard

The Sport Solo Group sold for $67.75 and included:

- front safety guard
- jiffy stand
- 5.00×16-inch wheels and tires
- stainless-steel air cleaner, timer cover, generator end cover, primary-chain-inspection cover, clutch cover, fork trim, foot-lever-bearing cover, and muffler shield
- colored shift ball
- chrome relay cover, headlight, taillight, rear fender tip, exhaust-pipe covers, rims, mirror and front chrome parking lamps
- deluxe solo saddle

The Utility Solo Group sold for $21.15 and included:

- black front safety guard
- air cleaner
- black wheels with 5.00×16-inch tires
- jiffy stand

The Utility Group for Sidecar Motorcycles sold for $15.60 and included:

- front safety guard
- stainless-steel air cleaner, chrome relay cover, timer cover, and generator end cover

The Standard Police Group sold for $69 and included:

- front safety guard
- jiffy stand
- 5.00×16-inch tires
- stainless-steel air cleaner, timer cover, and generator end cover
- chrome relay cover
- rear-wheel siren
- speedometer hand control
- police deluxe solo saddle

Factory Paint Options

The 1949 Panheads were available in four standard colors and one optional color. Standard at no extra charge were Burgundy (described as a "rich, deep maroon color"), Peacock Blue ("a beautiful green-blue"), Brilliant Black, and Police Silver (for police bikes only). Optional for $8 extra was Metallic Congo Green ("a deep, attractive green accented by the metallic pigments"). Only Brilliant Black and Police Silver were carried over from 1948.

Chassis Updates and Detail Changes

As mentioned in the introduction, hydraulic forks were the marquee change to the chassis for 1949, but there were also many others made to harmonize with the style of the front end.

Hydra-Glide Forks Why did Harley introduce telescopic forks when the old spring fork had worked so well for so long? Because springers actually really hadn't worked all that well at all

(having only 2 inches of stiff travel and needing continuous maintenance), and because most of the competition had switched to the new telescopics. From Harley's perspective, another tidal wave of thousands of Brit bikes with telescopic forks was about to wash over America's shores for 1949, so the Panhead needed an immediate suspension and image upgrade to keep from being swept aside.

So telescopics the Panhead got, but it got a set that could only have come from Milwaukee. Unlike the spindly-looking forks on the foreign bikes, the Hydra-Glide forks looked stout and

The horn used on the Hydra-Glides is the same one that had been mounted atop the fender of the spring-fork models, but it was now bolted to brackets welded onto the back of the front down tubes.

Early 1949 Hydra-Glide forks had lubrication fittings hidden under the domed caps shown here.

This still bike has the correct Air Flow front fender with spot-welded fender brackets (1950 and later fenders have riveted-on front-fender brackets). The spot-welded fenders tended to crack, so most have been replaced on the 1950 and later fenders with riveted fender brackets.

muscular. The fork legs were spaced wide to clear a fat front tire and a new front fender. The upper tubes and whole top of the fork assembly were shrouded in black-painted, stamped-steel cover panels that gave the front end the massive good looks that are still so much a part of Harley style. Polished stainless-steel covers were optional, but the bright covers looked so good that few bikes were ordered with the plain-Jane black ones.

The front cover panel had four horizontal stripes relief-embossed on each side of the headlight. This front panel style was used through

1954. The name "Hydra-Glide" was stamped into the top front panel on 1950–1959 models, but it is possible that some late-1949 fork panels were so stamped. The fork tubes were made of chrome-moly steel, and the sliders of heat-treated sand-cast aluminum that was then painted black. Sand-cast sliders are a 1949-only item. Later sliders were die-cast and were available in painted or polished form.

Ads for the 1949 Panhead emphasized that the new forks were not just about looks, however. "Hydra-Glide sets a new standard in smooth-as-flying, road-hugging comfort . . ." said one, and the ad copy was right. Hydra-Glide forks gave more than twice the travel of the spring forks and their velocity-sensitive valving tamed bumpy roads much better than the old spring forks. Along with the new fork came a much larger and more powerful front brake.

Several modifications introduced during the Hydra-Glide's first year attest that it wasn't as entirely trouble-free as advertised. Early in the production run, Harley introduced vented, domed caps covering the oil fittings. Late in the production run, a new vented cap was introduced without the oil fitting. In this configuration, the forks were produced almost unchanged through 1959.

A new, friction-operated steering damper mounted atop the steering stem of the forks. Turning its large, starfish-shaped, stamped-steel knob increased or decreased (depending on the direction it was turned) the pressure on the unit's spider spring. This style of steering damper was used through 1959.

Handlebars and Controls Those new forks were fitted with updated handlebars and control spirals. Spring-fork handlebars had been rigidly attached to the top fork plate, so the handlebars lacked adjustment capability. The new Hydra-Glide bar was a one-piece tubular bar clamped to the top fork bracket by a handlebar riser, making the handlebars adjustable to accommodate rider preference. Standard handlebars were solid-mounted Speedster (short) bars. Longer Buckhorn bars were available as a no-cost option. All solid-mounted bars and their risers were painted black. Control coils from the spirals and wires from the horn and light switches were routed out a slot in the bottom of the center section of the handlebar, through a phenolic resin housing between the handlebar and fork top cover, and through the fork top cover. The electrical wires attached to a terminal block behind the fork cowling, and the control coils were routed to the carburetor and circuit-breaker.

Chrome-plated rubber-mounted bars (really rubber-mounted risers) were optional for an additional $18.75, in Speedster or Buckhorn

Not all 1949 Panheads were Hydra-Glides. Harley-Davidson had learned from hard experience not to force change on its customers, so it offered the 1949 Panhead with spring forks. This FLP (the "P" is the designator for spring-fork Panheads) is ostensibly one of 486 that H-D records show were built that year. Harley recommended that motorcycles for use with sidecars or package trucks be purchased with the spring forks, because the Hydra-Glide fork angle was too steep for good stability with a sidecar attached. The company also recommended that all solo machines be ordered with the Hydra-Glide fork because of its superior ride quality. Even so, H-D sold some sidecar bikes with Hydra-Glide forks and some other solo machines with the spring forks.

style. They could also be ordered from the 1949 Accessory Catalog for $35. At the time the new 1949 bikes were delivered, all rubber-mounted bars and risers were chrome plated, and all solid-mounted bars and risers were painted black. But after delivery, an owner could install Harley-Davidson or aftermarket chrome-plated bars into the solid-mounted risers. Rubber-mounted bars were also optional for spring-fork models for an additional $23.

The solid-mounted risers and the early-1949 rubber-mounted risers use two separate riser "towers" with top clamps. Two screws cinch each top clamp over the handlebar, securing the bar to the riser tower, and one center bolt clamps each tower to the top fork bracket. Risers for rubber-mounted bars have a rubber bushing with a steel sleeve through the center of each riser and a rubber bushing under each riser tower.

Stainless steel was used in many new places for 1949. The rocker covers and air-cleaner cover were made of stainless for 1949, and the rocker covers would remain stainless through 1956, while the air-cleaner covers would remain stainless through 1965. On Hydra-Glide models, polished stainless upper fork covers were available as an option (standard covers are black-painted steel).

The new rubber-mounted bars reduced vibration felt through the handlebars, but the steering feel became very "loose" if the riser bolts were not very tightly clamped or the rubber bushings were worn. Harley fixed the problem by adding a chromed-steel riser link plate on all bikes with rubber-mounted bars produced as of April 7, 1949. Harley also issued *Shop Dope* No. 287 to offer free parts and instructions to retrofit the new riser link on all earlier Hydra-Glides with rubber-mounted bars. The company evidently saw the problem as serious because it urged "prompt action" in retrofitting the new parts.

Linking the two riser towers at the top, this new plate helped create a nearly flex-free mounting between the bars and the top fork bracket, while still retaining the vibration-reducing qualities of rubber-mounted risers. The two mounting screws that had been used to secure each handlebar clamp were replaced (on the new bikes and with the parts in the retrofit kit) by two studs with acorn nuts, allowing tighter clamping of all parts. Solid-mounted bars were not fitted with the new riser link.

The new bars also included changes to accommodate the new-style spirals introduced in 1949 (two threaded screw holes 180 degrees apart on each bar for the spiral-retainer screws.)

1949's spirals looked markedly different from the controls they replaced. The new spirals use a shorter twist sleeve held on by a chrome-plated retainer on the inboard end. Two screws secure the retainer to the handlebar. The grips are now 4 ½ inches long and do not have end holes for the spiral end screws. This style of spiral was used through 1953.

As before, the right spiral controls the throttle, and the left spiral controls the spark advance. The new style of controls was also used on the spring-fork Panheads for 1949, so a genuine 1949 springer model will have the new-style spirals. A fake one will likely have the 1948 forks, bars, and spirals in place of the 1949's Hydra-Glide forks and new-style bars. The new spirals were used on all Panheads from 1949 to 1953.

Larger Headlight All Hydra-Glide models received a larger, more powerful headlight to go with the new forks. The new 8.19-inch bulb was a sealed-beam (called "sealed ray" by Harley-Davidson) type with 32 candlepower for both low and high beam. Its low beam "dipped to the right" and aimed lower than the high beam. Harley claimed that the new light put out 10–13 percent more light than the old. As *The Enthusiast* stated,

"Better and more light for night riding is good." True enough.

The new light was housed in a stamped housing that mounted to a bracket on the fork lower bracket. The bulb is held in the shell by a retaining ring that fastens to the housing with three screws. The brightly polished headlamp door covered the retaining ring and the edge of the light, tidying up the look of the headlamp unit.

Like the fork covers, the headlight housing was painted black on standard bikes, but was chrome plated for bikes ordered with the Deluxe Solo Group or the Sport Solo Group. The chrome headlight could also be ordered separately for $2.30 extra. This style of headlight was used through 1959.

Springer models for 1949 retained the old-style, 7-inch headlight with "pre-focused" 21/32-candlepower bulb and separate reflector and front lens.

Revised Frames On Hydra-Glide-equipped bikes, the horn, which had been mounted on the spring forks, was moved to the front of the frame, mounted between the two down tubes. On early-1949 frames, square-cornered brackets were welded to the backs of the down tubes. On later-1949 frames, the down tubes were slightly flattened on the back side where the horn mounts were welded. The horn is the same horn that had been used on the spring-fork models. It was painted black, but chrome covers could be ordered to dress it up. The horn button was mounted on the left bar.

Spring-fork bikes appear to have been fitted with leftover 1948 frames or new-production 1948-style frames (these frames lack the new horn-mount blocks and the down tubes are not flattened for these blocks).

In the interest of bearing longevity and obtaining "effortless ease of handling," Harley-Davidson engineers used tapered Timken roller bearings in the steering head for 1949. Each bearing used 15 0.383-inch-long Timken rollers instead of the 17 ball bearings used top and bottom in 1948.

New "Air Flow" Fenders Restyled front and rear fenders were fitted to 1949 Hydra-Glide models. Spring-fork bikes were fitted with the old-style front fender and the new-style rear fender.

New front fenders were stamped from a single sheet of 20-gauge steel and had deep, streamlined skirts, though not nearly as deep as those on the Indian motorcycles. Harley-Davidson named the new-style fenders "Air Flow."

Streamlined brackets were spot-welded to the fender skirt on each side to mount the handsome new front fender to the fork sliders. The Air Flow front fender was a hit with riders, both for its styling

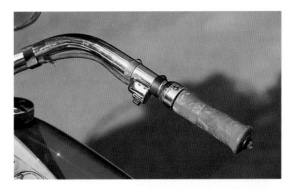

Top: All the 1949 Panheads, even those with the spring forks, were fitted with the new-style spirals. These spirals have a longer grip than the 1948 spirals and are held to the bar by the chrome retaining ring inboard of the grip (the old spirals had been held on by an end nut that threaded into the end of the handlebar).

Bottom: Shown is the correct speedometer for all Panheads from 1948–1952. The recessed center panel was painted bluish gray and enclosed the odometer and trip meter. Odometer numerals are black on a white background; odometer numerals are black for miles and red for tenths, both on a white background. Numbers are painted in off-white on the underside of the glass. The H-D bar and shield is painted on the underside of the glass in white, toward the rear. The pointer is red, and the bezel is chrome plated. Chrome-plated instrument panels were not offered in 1949.

and for the excellent protection it offered. All was not perfect, however. The fenders often cracked at the spot welds, so new fenders were released in late 1949 or early 1950 with riveted-on brackets. Many restored 1949 Hydra-Glides have the later, riveted brackets because their original fenders failed in use and were replaced (under warranty, or later by the owner) with the riveted fenders.

New, stainless-steel tips wrapped around the sides of the Air Flow front fender, stretching back almost to the fork sliders. The design on the new fender tip continues the lines of the ribbed tire tread, adding a distinct, modern look to the fender. This style of tip was standard on all Hydra-Glides through 1956. A thin stainless-steel trim stripe at the fender's rear edge was standard on all Hydra-Glides through 1957. The front fender light that had been optional on spring-fork Pans

"Van," presumably the original owner of this machine, went all out in decorating it. It has the correct 1949–1952 style Deluxe Buddy Seat (red rosettes under the nickel stars), the optional seat rail that was new for 1949, and the King Size saddlebags. It is also fitted with many other aftermarket and accessory-catalog items, including a chrome shifter ball, chrome instrument cover, chrome fork-spring covers, chrome safety bars (chrome safety bars were not available on new machines until 1950), and too many others to list.

was not offered for the Air Flow fenders, although it could still be ordered on spring-fork machines.

Later in 1949, an accessory "roller" chrome front bumper was offered. This assembly consisted of a tapered-cylinder bumper spanning two bumper rods that mounted to the fender with two cylindrical lugs apiece. This bumper was a $5.75 option that really dressed up the fender and offered a modest degree of protection. No other front-fender trim was offered on new Hydra-Glides for 1949. Spring-fork-equipped Panheads could be ordered with the optional fender tip and fender light.

Rear fenders were stamped in two pieces (front and rear) that were joined together by a hinge that allowed the rear portion of the fender to be pivoted upward during tire changes. The tomb-stone-style taillight was carried over from the old-style rear fender, except that the integral license-plate bracket was riveted on, rather than attached by screws. The taillight body was painted black on standard models but a chrome-plated taillight was available for the bargain price of 95¢, or when the Deluxe Solo Group or Sport Solo Group was ordered.

Three stainless-steel "sergeant stripes" wrapped around from the edge of the wheel well to the taillight. Three vertical ribs were stamped into the chain recess on the left side of the fender, but some early-1949 rear fenders lacked the ribs on the chain recess. The rear fender with sergeant stripes and the three ribs were fitted on 1949 and 1950 Panheads only.

For those who wanted to further dress up their rear fender, a chrome rear-fender tip (the same one that had been offered in 1948) and a chrome rear bumper were offered. The Deluxe Solo Group and Sport Solo Group included the chrome rear-fender tip, or was available separately for $2.35. The bumper was available in the Deluxe Solo Group, or separately for $6.95.

Larger Front Brake Front brakes on most bikes of the late 1940s are so weak as to border on useless, and the one Harley had used on its springer models was among the weakest. For 1949, Harley-Davidson engineers made an attempt at improving the situation by introducing a larger and more powerful front brake for the

Hydra-Glide. Spring-fork models made do with the old front brake.

Harley's new Hydra-Glide front brake was an all-new design with an 8-inch drum (the old drums were 7¼ inches) and an internal brake-actuating lever (the old brakes had an external actuating lever). Its cast-iron drum was painted black and attached to the star-shaped wheel hub with five screws (front and rear wheels were still interchangeable). The backing plate was cast aluminum and attached to the left fork leg. The brake backing plate is unpolished on 1949 machines. The new, larger, ⅛-inch brake cable was housed in a flexible coil from the left hand lever to the back side of the lower steering stem. The cable was then housed in a steel tube that carried it along the left side of the fender to where the tube attached to a boss on the top edge of the brake backing plate. The cable routed inside the brake drum to the actuating lever, and a pull on the hand lever pivoted the actuating arm, which rotated the cam, expanding the two identical brake shoes outward to contact the inner surface of the drum.

The Harley-Davidson ads claimed the new brake had 34 percent more braking surface than the old brake. Even so, it still felt anemic compared to the rear brake and—despite Harley's claims of "instant stopping power"—the front brake was only marginally adequate for a 600-pound motorcycle. To be fair, though, it was as good as any other front brake of the era, except the two-sided drum brake used on the Vincents, so Harley-Davidson used the new front-brake assembly almost without change through the end of the Panhead line.

Motor Updates

In addition to all the chassis changes, Harley-Davidson made a few minor changes to the power plant to correct faults and complement the new running gear.

Intake-Valve Oiling Perhaps the most significant addition was that of an oil-supply spigot that cured forever the 1948 Panheads' problem with oil-starved intake-valve stems. The spigot picked up oil from the rocker bearing and dripped it on the intake-valve spring, from which it splashed onto the valve stem to reduce valve-guide wear and keep the valve from sticking.

Silver-Painted Cylinders A new silver-silicone paint finish improved the appearance of the cylinders and made them look like they were cast of aluminum alloy. "Organo-silicon oxide polymers" in this special paint gave it the ability to resist heat and rust formation far better than the high-temperature paints previously used. All

Panhead cylinders from 1949 through 1965 were painted silver-silicone.

Carburetors Updated carburetors and new breaker points made by Harley-Davidson were fitted to improve everyday rideability. The 1949 61 bikes were fitted with the Linkert M-36 carburetor with a 1⅛-inch venturi. Early 1949 74 bikes were also fitted with the M-36, but later-1949 to early-1950 74 bikes were fitted with the M-45 carburetor with a 1 5/16-inch venturi. During the 1949 production run, the material used to make the intake manifold was changed to cast iron (it had been made of steel tubing), but the finish remained cadmium plated.

Silver-Painted Pipes and Mufflers All exhaust pipes on the 1949 Big Twins were coated with the same silver-silicone paint used on the cylinders, and the mufflers were painted in a black-silicone paint. The new paint proved far more resistant to rust than the previous high-temperature black

The rear fender of the 1949 springer Panheads is the same as the one on Hydra-Glide bikes. The tombstone taillight is correct for 1948–1954 Panheads. Standard taillight bodies and lens doors were painted black; chrome-plated taillights were optional. Correct taillight lenses feature the Harley-Davidson name curving along the top, as shown. The rear bumper shown was a new option for 1949 and retailed for $6.95. The rear fender tip shown is probably an aftermarket item (the correct tip is the "bombardier" tip).

Tank emblems on 1947–1950 Harleys were designed by famed designer Brooks Stevens. Both the circle at the front and the lettering should be painted red (these reproduction emblems have black-painted letters).

Harley-Davidson designers created another instant classic in the Hydra-Glide. With black-painted sliders and brightly polished stainless-steel trim everywhere you look, the first-year Hydra-Glide was perhaps the best looking of the breed.

paint used on the pipes and mufflers for 1948 and earlier twins.

Many owners opted for the chrome pipe covers to dress up the header pipes (available for $3.85 or as part of the Deluxe Solo and Sport Solo groups) and the stainless-steel muffler cover (available for $5.75 or as part of the Deluxe Solo and Sport Solo groups). Chrome exhaust pipes and mufflers are sometimes seen on restorations of 1949 bikes but are incorrect. The standard, single-exhaust header pipes were painted in silver-silicone through 1965. The S-pipe and Y-pipe were painted silver-silicone for 1949–50, but were chrome plated for 1951 and after.

Stainless-Steel Madness

For 1949, even the standard Utility Solo Group bikes were fitted with an unusual assortment of chromed and stainless-steel parts, including a stainless generator end cover, a chromed generator-relay cover, and a stainless-steel ignition-timer cover. These parts had been painted on 1948 and would again be painted on 1950 utility models.

Several other parts that had been chrome plated on base-model machines in 1948 were changed to polished stainless-steel for 1949. Most prominent among these are the rocker covers and the air-cleaner cover. Stainless rocker covers would be standard through 1956, and stainless air-cleaner covers would be standard through 1965.

Other parts that had been optional in chrome-plated form for 1948 were made of stainless steel for 1949 only. These include the primary-chain inspection plate, the clutch inspection plate, and the foot-lever-bearing cover, all of which were painted on the base-model bikes. These parts were changed back to chrome plated on the 1950 option groups.

Finally, the optional muffler cover was made of stainless steel. As far as I have been able to determine, this is a 1949-only part, because I have seen no optional muffler cover listed on the Harley-Davidson order blanks for 1948 (though I have seen stainless-steel covers on original 1948 Panheads), and because a new muffler style was introduced in 1950.

Options and Accessories
The most popular accessories for 1949 were basically the same as in previous years: saddlebags, windshield, front spotlights, parking lamps, Deluxe Solo or Deluxe Buddy seat, rear safety guard, and chrome bits—but new models of many of these familiar accessories were introduced, as well as an optional 20-amp output radio generator.

Optional Radio Generator Two-way radios became more common on police bikes after World War II, and the old Model 32E2R radio generator wasn't up to the job. It could usually supply enough current, but it often would overheat in the process, burning out the armature. For 1949, Harley-Davidson engineers installed the new Model 48 generator. This new generator was capable of 20-amp output (versus 15 amps for the older radio generator) and was fitted with an integral cooling fan attached to the armature shaft. A voltage regulator was fitted to a special bracket on the left side of the bike.

Windshield and Rear Safety Guard The optional windshield was redesigned to wrap around the Hydra-glide forks. The new windshield attached to the side of the fork (rather than to the handle-bars), had Plexiglas lower panels (rather than vinyl), and sold for $17.75. An adjustable panel over the head light could be raised or lowered to adjust air flow to the rider. All panels were clear Plexiglas through 1955, but blue or red lower panels were offered for 1956 and later models.

The rear safety guard was the same as the 1948 Panhead and was offered only painted black (chrome-plated rear safety guards were first offered on new bikes in 1950).

Spotlight Mounts and Parking Lamps New front spotlight mounts were designed for the Hydra-Glide front end. The individual lamps are the same as for 1948, but the lights mount to separate brackets attached to the sides of the fork (rather than to a light bar). Spotlights could be ordered for $17. The lamps were used through 1961, but the new mounts only through 1959.

As a replacement for the front-fender light on the spring-fork models, new bullet-shaped front parking lamps were introduced. These lights were chrome plated and mounted to the sides of the fork, looking much like a turn signal. They had a clear lens and sold for $4.75 per pair (they were also included in the Deluxe Solo and Sport Solo groups). Rear parking lamps were also offered, and these rear lights were the same as the front, except with red lenses. They sold for $5.50 a pair.

Seat and Saddlebags The Deluxe Solo Seat was the same style of seat that had been used in 1948, and was available for $11 (in place of the standard saddle). It was also included as part of the Deluxe Solo and Sport Solo groups. The Deluxe Buddy Seat for 1949 was the same as the 1948 version, except with red plastic rosettes instead of yellow, and a new, one-piece chrome handrail was optional. The buddy seat could be ordered for $16 (also in place of the standard saddle).

The optional King Size saddlebags were the same as for 1948, and cost $37.50 when ordered separately. They were also included in the Deluxe Solo Group.

Production for 1949
Harley-Davidson experienced a great sales year in 1949. The company sold 12,685 Panheads (239 fewer than in 1948). As expected, Hydra-Glide models dominated sales. The best-selling model was the Hydra-Glide FL, at 8,014 sold, followed by the Hydra-Glide EL at 3,419. Despite Harley's recommendation against using the Hydra-Glide motorcycles with a sidecar, 177 ES and 490 FS Hydra-Glide sidecar models were sold. A total of 585 other buyers, apparently, opted against the Hydra-Glide front end, resulting in sales of 99 ELP and 486 FLP spring-fork Panheads.

These production figures for sidecar- and spring-fork-equipped machines must be viewed as highly suspect, in my opinion. Harley-Davidson officially peddled the Models EP and FP with spring forks for use on all sidecar rigs—yet not one of these models is listed as having been sold! Meanwhile, the sales list includes 667 Models ES and FS Hydra-Glide sidecar bikes—which Harley-Davidson actively discouraged its customers from buying—and 585 Models ELP and FLP solo springer bikes—which many enthusiasts and dealers insist were never offered for sale.

A gorgeous 1950 Hydra-Glide restored by Elmer Ehnes. Note the new-style Mellow-Tone muffler, which was used through 1951, and the unpainted fork sliders. Standard mufflers were painted black and had Parkerized hangers. Optional mufflers were chrome plated and had stainless-steel hangers. This is a beautiful restoration, but it has a few non-stock items, such as the whitewall tires and later-style solo seat specified by the owner.

Would so many customers really ignore Harley-Davidson's recommendations, and would the factory really comply if the customers did? My answer to both questions: I don't think so.

So how do I explain it? My best guess is that the sales figures for the springer models actually represents a composite of the relatively large number of spring-fork sidecar bikes, and whatever small number of spring-fork solo bikes were actually built, and that the sales figures listed for the sidecar bikes actually represent a composite of the relatively large number of spring-fork machines and the relatively small number of Hydra-Glide-equipped sidecar bikes. Such duplication in Harley-Davidson's official figures is commonplace, especially for wartime figures.

The 1950 Hydra-Glides

After so many changes in each of the previous two years, Harley's designers made do with subtle changes for model year 1950. Most important,

perhaps, was the introduction of an adjustable-trail fork, because that gave Harley-Davidson the freedom to retire the springer front end on its overhead-valve twins until it was revived in updated form for the Springer Softail of 1988.

Models, Prices, and Option Groups

For 1950, two basic versions of the Hydra-Glide were offered in each displacement size, the 61 models E and EL and the 74 models F and FL. In addition, sidecar gearing could be ordered on the E and F, making the ES and FS models. Per usual Harley-Davidson practice, however, only the "E" or the "F," not the "S," was stamped into the case as part of the serial number. All were fitted with Hydra-Glide forks.

Base-model 61s carried a retail price of $735, and the 74s carried a retail price of $750. Both prices were unchanged from 1949. Also per usual Harley-Davidson practice, these prices were misleading because all new 1950 Hydra-Glides were shipped with one of three solo option groups, one sidecar group, or one police group, which added to the cost.

The Deluxe Solo Group sold for $95.50 and consisted of the following items: chrome front safety guard, air cleaner, 5.00x16-inch wheels and tires, jiffy stand, chrome shift ball, chrome headlight, chrome taillight, chrome rims, stainless fork trim, chrome exhaust-pipe covers, chrome muffler, chrome clutch inspection cover, chrome timer cover, chrome primary-chain inspection cover, polished fork sliders and brake side cover, pair of King Size saddlebags, and chrome rear safety guard.

The Sport Solo Group sold for $53.70 and included the following items:
- chrome front safety guard
- air cleaner
- 5.00x16-inch wheels and tires
- jiffy stand
- chrome shift ball, headlight, taillight, rims, exhaust-pipe covers, muffler, clutch cover, timer cover, and primary-chain-inspection cover
- stainless fork trim
- polished fork sliders and brake side cover

The Utility Solo Group sold for $19.95 and included:

- black front safety guard
- air cleaner
- black wheels with 5.00x16-inch tires
- jiffy stand

The Utility Group for Sidecar Motorcycles sold for $15.60 and included:
- black front safety guard
- air cleaner
- black wheels with 5.00x16-inch tires

In addition, Harley-Davidson recommended that all motorcycles ordered for sidecar use be equipped with the optional changeable-trail fork, for an additional $7. Better not take off the sidecar, though, because the bike wouldn't even have a jiffy stand.

The Standard Police Group sold for $67.90 and included:
- black front safety guard
- jiffy stand
- black wheels with 5.00x16-inch tires
- air cleaner
- rear-wheel siren
- speedometer hand control, and
- police deluxe solo saddle

This sparkling 1950 Hydra-Glide is fitted with the adjustable-rake forks that were new for 1950. By loosening a couple bolts and pulling the forks forward, an owner could rake out the forks to increase stability when the bike was used with a sidecar. Because of this feature, the spring forks were no longer offered as an option. Shown is the correct Deluxe Buddy Seat and King Size saddlebags with plain-style buckles (the piping on the bags should be red, however).

Top: This style of speedometer was used on civilian Panheads from 1948 through 1952.

Bottom: All Panheads for 1950 were Hydra-Glides. The forks themselves differed from the early ones in having the name "Hydra-Glide" embossed into the front panel and the hex top caps shown here.

Factory Paint Options The 1950 Panheads were available in four standard colors and four optional colors. Standard at no extra charge were Brilliant Black, Ruby Red, Riviera Blue, and Police Silver (for police bikes only). Optional for $10 extra were Metallic Green, Flight Red, Azure Blue, and White.

Chassis Updates and Detail Changes

As already mentioned, Hydra-Glides for 1950 were little changed from the 1949 models, returning with the streamlined tank emblem and sergeant stripes on the rear fender. But many small changes did distinguish the 1950 Hydra-Glide from the 1949 model.

Adjustable-Trail Fork The reason the old spring forks were no longer offered on Panheads was because an adjustable-trail version of the Hydra-Glide forks was available (for $5 extra) for use on sidecar and package-truck motorcycles.

Externally, there were few clues to distinguish the adjustable forks from the fixed-rake Hydra-Glide forks. The easiest way to spot adjustable

forks is to look at their top cover near the handlebar risers. If two large chrome plugs stick up above the cover outboard of the risers, the fork is the fixed-rake model. If the top cover is smooth, without showing the plugs, the fork is most likely the adjustable model—not necessarily, though, because fixed-rake 1958 and 1959 Servi-car forks are also smooth on top and may have been retrofitted to some Panheads.

Adjustability was built into the lower fork bracket. Loosen two bolts in the lower bracket, and you can change the position of the bracket two ways in relation to the steering stem: solo or raked for sidecar.

Additional Front-End Changes The fork sliders for 1950 and later forks were die cast for a smoother appearance, and were not painted. For an extra $3.50 at the time of order, the factory would polish the sliders and brake backing plate. The polished sliders and backing plate were also included in the Deluxe Solo and Sport Solo groups.

Spot-welded brackets on 1949 Hydra-Glide front fenders had proved so troublesome that the 1950 and later brackets were riveted on (with five rivets on each side). The new fenders proved better able to resist cracking.

Sometime during the 1949 or 1950 production run, the factory began stamping the name "Hydra-Glide" in the angled V-panel at the top end of the front fork panel. This new panel with Hydra-Glide and the four horizontal stripes on each side of the headlight was used through 1954.

Internally, the 1950 forks were updated with six baffle plates and a new breather valve. These updates prevented air from being trapped in the forks, and the baffle plates prevented oil from being pumped out the breather.

Odds and Ends To prevent chafing that caused premature failure of the front brake cable, a larger diameter (⅜-inch) upper tube was introduced for 1950. In tandem, the adjusting screw on the new cable was increased to 5⁄16 inch.

Lastly, the gas lines were given rubber mounts at the gas tank and carburetor ends to reduce the chance of the gas line developing a crack from vibration.

Motor Updates

Though the motor updates for 1950 were relatively minor, Harley-Davidson designers did attempt to give the Panhead engine more "zoom and steam" by designing new cylinder heads. These heads featured larger intake ports that Harley claimed were good for a 10-percent boost in power.

Other changes were made, too. Gone was the plugged hole that was near each exhaust port on the 1948–1949 heads. Also, new numbers—"119 50 FRONT" or "119 501 REAR"—were cast in relief into the underside of the head between the pushrod holes. These castings were used through 1954.

Bronze exhaust-valve guides (replacing steel guides) were introduced on the new head castings and were fitted to all 1950–January 1957 motors.

Carburetors Feeding the new cylinder heads on 1950 models were recalibrated versions of the M-36 (on 61 models) and M-45 (on 74 models) carburetors used in 1949. Updates to these carburetors included a fixed jet, "limited" adjustability of the high-speed needle, and a larger accelerating well. The result was better throttle response and the ability to more quickly fine-tune the carburetor. To denote the changes, the new carbs were designated M-36A and M-45A.

About mid-year, the 61 models were fitted with the new M-61 carburetor, which had a 1⅛-inch venturi. The M-61 carburetor was used on the 61s through 1952. Late in 1950, the 74 models were fitted with the M-74 carburetor with 1⁵⁄₁₆-inch venturi, and this carburetor was standard until it was superseded by the M-74B carburetor during the 1951 season.

These carburetors worked so well that Harley-Davidson offered a program to update the earlier carburetors. If the earlier carburetors and a conversion fee of $5 were returned to the company by a dealer, Harley would return an M-36A or M-61 carburetor (for M-36 carbs that were returned) or an M-45A or M-74 carburetor (for M-45 carbs that were returned).

Mellow-Tone Muffler For 1950, the old "rocket-fin" muffler was replaced by a new tubular muffler that tapered to a straight pipe at each end. Harley-Davidson named it the "Mellow-Tone" muffler after its deeper, more mellow exhaust note. Like the 1949 muffler, this muffler was painted silicone-black on standard bikes. Unlike the 1949 muffler, it was available in a chrome-plated finish for $3.50 extra, or as part of the Deluxe Solo and Sport Solo groups.

Oil Filter The oil filter was a popular option on the Panhead since its introduction in 1948. Those early oil filters attached directly to the oil-return fitting on the oil tank. For 1950, a revised oil filter was introduced that mounted the chrome-plated filter away from the oil tank to isolate it from vibration. The updated filter was supported by a mounting arm to the frame and was connected to the oil tank by a short metal return tube. A mounting stud in the cap of the new filter secured the filter housing to the mounting arm. According to *Shop Dope* No. 305 (issued on April 4, 1950), a conversion kit was offered to convert the earlier oil-tank-mounted

filter to the new frame-mounted filter. The kit was priced at $1.50.

Engine Minutiae For restorers and others who revel in fine detail, the gear-cover screws were changed to Phillips-head type for 1950 and 1951. They were still cadmium plated, however. Beginning in 1950 and continuing through mid-1953, straight-slot and Phillips-head screws were used interchangeably during production to fasten the tappet blocks to the right crank case (only straight-slot screws had been used in 1948 and 1949). For all 1950–1964 Panheads, the screws that fasten the outer primary cover to the inner cover were Parkerized filister-head screws with Phillips slots (they had previously had straight slots).

Another subtle change was made to the outer primary cover, to the mounting area for the primary-chain-inspection cover. The mounting screws for the inspection cover were drilled at 6 o'clock and at 12 o'clock (they had been at 3 o'clock and 9 o'clock on 1949 and earlier covers). The standard chain and clutch inspection covers were still painted black to match the finish of the outer primary cover, but the optional inspection covers were now chrome-plated steel, rather than polished

The right side of the 1950 EL shows the 1949–1954 fork top and the front panel with four horizontal stripes and the name "Hydra-Glide" embossed into the cover. The oil filter shown was introduced in 1950 to isolate the filter from vibration. It features a short oil pipe connecting the filter to the oil tank, and a mounting arm to the frame is bolted to a stud in the filter cap.

The screws that fasten the primary-chain inspection cover are at six and twelve o'clock. This positioning was new for 1950 (the screws had been at three and nine) and was used through 1954, the last year for the "diamond" style primary cover. Also note the rivets that fasten the fender brackets and the thin, stainless trim strip at the lower rear edge of the fender. This strip was standard from 1949 to 1957.

stainless steel. Stainless steel was also discontinued for the generator end cover. Panhead generator end covers were all painted black for 1950–1954 (from 1955–mid-1959, they are all cadmium plated).

Detail Changes
The 1950 model year saw a limited number of detail changes. Harley-Davidson offered a "neater" Deluxe Solo Seat and slightly varied saddlebags and front safety guards.

Seat and Saddlebags For 1950, the seam style on the optional Deluxe Solo Seat was revised for a neater appearance. The cut ends of the leather were no longer visible where the leather seat cover is stitched to the leather piece that is riveted to the seat pan, because the edge of the seat cover wraps around and underneath the cut end of the bottom leather, and the stitching goes through all three layers of leather. The Deluxe Solo Seat was a very popular option and cost an additional $7.50 at the time of order.

The black King Size leather saddlebags for 1950 were the same as 1948–1949 except that the piping was available in red or white (instead

of orange; the white piping was a running change made during the 1950 production year) and the buckles were plain-style (buckle frames are uniform in thickness on all edges, unlike the oblong "Western" buckles used on previous bags). Another running change was the addition of fringed King Size saddlebags with white leather fringe around the bottom edge of the cover and side.

New, smaller bags were introduced during the 1950 model year for the 45 models, but they were also available for installation on the Big Twins. The Streamliner saddlebags were a more compact bag with orange plastic piping (at the top edge of the cover, at the lower edge of the cover, and at the edge of the sides) and a complex pattern of decoration, including nickel dots on the top of the cover, three Z-shaped designs of ten nickel dots each on the side of the cover, a single row of nickel dots along the lower edge of the sides of the bag, three leather straps with nickel buckles, and an oval nickel piece to each side of the center buckle. Nickel dots were arranged around the nickel ovals and in three single rows sweeping down and back from the ovals. This bag was offered in 1950 and 1951 (in 1952, the color of the piping was changed to red).

Front Safety Guard Nothing was changed about the front safety guard on the Panhead except that for the first time it was offered in chrome-plated finish from the factory. The plated guard was available at the time of order for an additional $3.60 or as part of the Deluxe Solo and Sport Solo groups. Standard front safety guards were painted black.

Production for 1950

Harley-Davidson sold 10,265 Hydra-Glides for 1950: 7,407 FL, 544 FS, 2,046 EL, and 268 ES. With a price only $15 greater than for 61 models, the 74 models continued to widen their sales lead over the 61 models.

Overall, though, Panhead sales were down by more than 20 percent compared to 1949, and many factors contributed to the decline. Indian had introduced a new Chief with hydraulic forks and a motor that was stroked to 80 cubic inches, and Indian dealers' floors were well stocked with the Norton, Matchless, Royal Enfield, Vincent, and other popular British bikes distributed in America by the Indian Sales Corporation. Triumph was experiencing such great success with its larger, U.S.-targeted models that it was gearing up to open an East Coast warehouse and distribution center to augment the West Coast-based Johnson Motors. As a final stroke of bad luck, some of Harley-Davidson's best customers had been recalled to service and sent off to the Korean War.

The most important immediate reason for the decline, however, was that pent-up demand from the war and postwar years had finally been satisfied. All the traditional Harley-Davidson customers who could afford to had replaced their earlier machines. The most important reason for the long-term decline to come was that Harley-Davidson was unable to, or didn't want to, serve the needs of the only market segments that were experiencing rapid growth—the so-called outlaw riders and sport riders.

Uniformed riding clubs and fully dressed bikes were going the way of the dinosaurs while the "chopper" and "biker" cults were rapidly growing. Harley actively discouraged their dealers from serving these new rebels, so a lively underground of unfranchised shops and after-market parts manufacturers began to grow. Harley's future was being shaped even though it chose not to participate.

Second, Harley-Davidson really wasn't adapting its Big Twin to make it appeal to customers for more refined or sporting machines, as Triumph and the other foreign makers were doing. Harley had made the Panhead a more civilized machine, but their engineers had not yet gone far enough. So despite Harley's best marketing efforts, sales would continue to decline until the next big

change was made (the high-performance FLH of 1955). Problem was, Harley-Davidson took so long to get there that even that next stage was only far enough to get some of their traditional clientele to upgrade to the new model—not nearly enough to win new converts. So it went for more than another decade.

The 1951 Hydra-Glides

Model year 1951 was a year of many small changes that updated the Hydra-Glide's look and subtly refined the whole package. The most important and lasting of these refinements came late in the year, when Harley-Davidson at last offered the option of foot shift and hand clutch on the Panhead.

Models, Prices, and Option Groups

For 1951, only the high-compression EL and FL were listed on the Harley-Davidson order blanks. Sidecar gearing could be ordered on the EL and FL, creating the ELS and FLS models. (Note: the low-compression 51E and 51F models are listed in the Model Descriptions section of *The Legend Begins*. Either Legend is in error, or these low-compression machines were special-order or export-only items.) Per usual Harley-Davidson practice, only EL or FL, not the "S," is stamped into the case as part of the serial number. All were fitted with Hydra-Glide forks.

Compensating, perhaps, for the lack of a price increase for 1950, prices for 1951 jumped by 20 percent. Base-model ELs carried a retail price of $885, and base-model FLs carried a retail price of $900. These prices were misleading, however, because all new Panheads were shipped with one of three solo option groups or one police group for 1951, which added to the cost.

The Deluxe Solo Group sold for $115 and included:
- chrome front and rear safety guards, headlight, taillight, rims, exhaust-pipe covers, muffler, clutch cover, timer cover, and chain-inspection cover
- air cleaner
- 5.00×16-inch wheels and tires
- jiffy stand
- colored shift ball
- stainless fork trim
- polished fork sliders and brake side cover
- pair of king-size saddle bags

The Sport Solo Group sold for $66.50 and included:
- chrome front safety guard
- air cleaner
- 5.00×16-inch wheels and tires
- jiffy stand

Harley-Davidson revised the Hydra-Glide for 1951 with new tank badges, reinforced handlebars, a new front crash bar, and many small engine updates.

The new tank badges featured the company name and an underline bar. This bike was fitted with a hand shift, but some late-1951 Hydra-Glides were fitted with a hand clutch and foot shift. D-ring reinforcements for the rocker covers were also new for 1951, but this bike has been updated with the later-style aluminum D-rings.

- colored shift ball
- chrome headlight, taillight, rims, exhaust-pipe covers, muffler, clutch cover, timer cover, and chain-inspection cover
- stainless fork trim
- polished fork sliders and brake side cover

The Utility Solo Group sold for $25.50 and included:

- black front safety guard
- air cleaner
- black wheels with 5.00x16-inch tires
- jiffy stand

The Standard Police Group sold for $78.75 and included:

- black front safety guard
- jiffy stand
- black wheels with 5.00x16-inch tires
- air cleaner
- rear-wheel siren
- speedometer hand control
- police deluxe solo saddle

Factory Paint Options Four standard and four optional colors were offered for 1951. Standard at no extra charge were Brilliant Black, Persian Red, Rio Blue, and Police Silver (for police bikes only). Optional for $10 extra were Metallic Green, Metallic Blue, and White. Harley-Davidson described the Persian Red, Metallic Green, and Metallic Blue as "a shade darker" than the Ruby Red, Metallic Green, and Azure Blue of 1950. The new Rio Blue is a shade lighter than the Riviera Blue of 1950.

Chassis Updates and Detail Changes

There were numerous updates and changes to the 1951 Panheads, the most important being the foot shift and hand clutch, which quietly emerged very late in the production year and without any of the fanfare Harley was known for.

First Foot-Shift Panheads Because the foot-shift update wasn't made official until 1952, we'll discuss it further in that section. Not many were made, but if you see a 1951 bike with a high serial number that has foot shift, it may indeed have had foot shift installed at the factory. This would be very difficult to document, however, because the "F" that denotes that the bike is a foot-shift model was never stamped on the motor as part of the serial number.

Gas-Tank Emblems The most apparent change was the fitting of new, two-piece gas-tank emblems. Gone were the Brooks Stevens-designed emblems used from 1947 to 1950, replaced by a chrome-plated brass emblem that featured the Harley-Davidson name in script with a separate underline bar, each piece fastened to the tank by three countersunk Phillips-head screws. These two-piece emblems were used through 1953, and the top, script portion was also retained for 1954 (the underline bar was deleted).

Rear Fender Trim on the rear fender was also changed for 1951. The three sergeant stripes astride the taillight were replaced by a single, wider stainless stripe on each side of the taillight. This stripe continues the line started by the side-trim pieces that flow back from the front-fender tip. This year's rear fender was also a one-year-only item, having both the three vertical channels pressed into the flat of the chain recess and the holes for mounting the new single-stripe trim pieces.

Adjustable-Rake Forks Adjustable-rake forks for use with sidecars and package trucks were revised for 1951. The two rake-adjustment bolts on the lower fork triple tree used in 1950 were replaced by a single longer bolt and nut, simplifying adjustment

Transmission The long rod from the shifter lever to the transmission was updated with the addition

Early-1951 Hydra-Glide frames had square-edged horn-mount blocks on the engine side of the down tubes, as shown here. Later in the year, round-edged mount blocks were substituted.

of a rod end at the transmission end (the old rod had a right-angle bend that engaged the transmission shifter lever). This rod end provided more positive shifting and a more durable connection than did the hooked end.

Frame A minor change to the frame was introduced in mid-1951. The horn-mount blocks were given rounded edges (rather than square edges). This frame was used only for 1951 (the frame for 1952 still had the rounded blocks, but had a new-style toolbox mount).

Handlebars Early Hydra-Glide handlebars had a large slot on the bottom of the tube's center, and the bars often cracked at this point—especially the solid-mounted bars because solid bars are exposed to greater vibration and were not equipped with the top riser link to reinforce the riser. That problem was solved for 1951 when new bars were introduced with a thick center-sleeve reinforcement. The optional rubber-mounted bars were chrome plated and the standard solid-mounted bars were painted black. These bars were used through the 1953 season.

For 1951, the three "sergeant stripes" on the rear fender were replaced by a single stripe.

A Touch of Chrome First, Harley-Davidson added a touch of chrome inside the motor with the fitting chrome-plated compression rings in the 1951 motors. These new rings were designed to reduce scuffing and wear during the critical break-in miles, helping to ensure that the cylinder walls remained smooth for a better ring seal.

For the first time, chrome-plated front-fender emblems with the name "Hydra-Glide" were offered as a $1.50 option for 1951. This nameplate was optional for 1951–1954.

Also, for the first time the S and Y exhaust pipes were chrome plated (rather than painted silver). Plated S- and Y-pipes are correct from 1951 on. The front and rear header pipes, however, were still painted with the aluminized silver-silicone paint.

Motor Updates

Model year 1951 was also a year of many small updates to the Panhead motor.

Camshaft A new camshaft was also fitted that incorporated ramps on the opening and closing sides of the lobe to smooth out valve action. These ramps worked in conjunction with new hydraulic lifters (designed for slower leak-down of oil) to reduce valve-train noise. The new cam was changed to a two-piece design with a separate gear pressed onto the camshaft.

Rocker Arms On early Panhead engines, the pressed-in pushrod ball sockets were known for working themselves loose, sometimes falling out, and sometimes causing oil starvation to the hydraulic lifters. The problem was fixed for good in 1951 when new rocker arms were introduced with the ball sockets machined right into them.

Gear Cover Casting The eight-rib style of gear cover was used again for 1951, but the surface of the casting was noticeably "rougher" in appearance because it was sand-cast, rather than die-cast. Its appearance further differed in that the ridge for the breather tunnel (which stretches diagonally from the lower rear corner to the upper center of the cover) and the outline of the pinion bushing were no longer visible. This cover bears the casting number 97-401 on the inside and has a cast-in breather baffle plate. This sand-cast, eight-rib cover is correct for 1951–1953 Pans. The gear cover is fastened by Phillips-head screws, but the generator mounting screws at the front of the cover are straight-slot screws for early 1951 bikes and Phillips head for later bikes. Phillips-head generator screws are correct on late-1951 to 1957 Panheads.

Carburetor Midway through the 1951 production run, 74 machines were fitted with an updated carburetor, the Linkert M-74B. This carburetor was used on the 74s through 1965.

Pinion Shaft Another midseason change was the substitution of a new pinion shaft slightly larger in diameter than the old shaft so that the pinion gear was a tighter-press fit over the shaft. This change was implemented at the factory on engine numbers higher than 51FL6137 and 51EL6976. The new shaft is identified by the 5/16-inch, left-hand-threaded hole in the shaft end that is plugged with a screw. This hole was provided for use with a new gear puller and installer tool that was necessary to remove or install the gear without damaging the flywheel assembly or bearings.

Near the very end of the 1951 production season, the factory began installing new, stronger piston pins with thicker-wall diameters.

Pushrod Tubes To cure chronic problems with oil leakage from the pushrod tubes, Harley-Davidson engineers introduced new pushrod-tube seals made of a "Neoprene-cork composition." The new seals weren't perfect, but they went a long way toward keeping the oil in the tubes and the dirt out.

D-Ring Reinforcement Harley-Davidson designers added chrome to the outside of the engine,
too, when they fitted "D-ring" reinforcements to
the rocker covers. The D-rings were named for
their D shape (which matched the shape of the
rocker cover's flanged edge). Each ring was made
of three ¹⁄₁₆-inch layers of sheet steel, spot-welded
together, chrome plated, and drilled for mounting screws. D-rings were made to evenly distrib-
ute the pressure applied by the mounting screws
over the entire surface of the rocker-cover flange,
preventing overtightened mounting screws from
distorting the edge of the cover and causing an
oil leak. Each D-ring and rocker cover were
secured by 12 mounting screws: 9 Phillips-head
screws and 3 Allen-head cap screws, each with
a lock washer. The Allen-head screws were used
on the three holes on the front side of the front
cylinder and the rear side of the rear cylinder
(the low points of each respective head) where
oil sometimes pooled above the gasket surface.
The seal had to be especially tight on these edges,
so Allen-head screws were used because they could
be tightened to a higher torque figure without
stripping than could the Phillips-head screws.

These new D-rings and screw combinations
sealed the rocker covers well and looked good, so
many owners of earlier Panheads have updated
their rocker covers with these D-rings. Even so,
the steel D-rings were original only on Panheads
built from 1951 to 1954.

The final change to the engine was a new
exhaust-port clamp. The old clamp was a plain
strap clamp made of stainless steel. The new
clamp was formed with a shoulder on one edge.
The shouldered edge is installed toward the head.

Options and Accessories
There were a few notable changes with options for
1951. Also, restorers will want to note that with
1951 Pans, transmission-cover screws were
changed to Phillips-head types, and in mid-1951
the generator-mounting screws were changed to
Phillips-head types.

Front Safety Guard The front safety guard was
strengthened for 1951 by forming it of one long
tube with a mounting bracket in the center and
on each end. The lower mounting brackets each
mounted to the frame by a single bolt. The

This Hydra-Glide has a
lot of extra chrome bits
that weren't available on
new 1951 machines, but
it shows the style set that
year, which was carried
forward into the
following years.

This style of speedometer was used for the last time in 1952. From the factory, dashes were painted the color of the tank—until 1957, when chrome dashes were first offered on new Hydra-Glides.

welded-on center bracket is fastened to the frame's upper front-safety-guard bracket by two bolts.

Generator A two-brush version of the Model 48 radio generator and a separate voltage regulator were fitted to radio-equipped police bikes for 1951. The third brush of the original Model 48 was discarded, and the remaining pair of brushes and the commutator were made 12.5 percent wider for longer life and greater current output. This is the only year the two-brush Model 48 was used.

Production for 1951
Sales of Harley-Davidson Big Twins continued their long slide for 1951: only 76 ES, 1,532 EL, 135 FS, and 6,560 FL Hydra-Glides were sold, a total of 8,303. Compare this figure to the more than 12,000 Panheads that had been sold in 1948, and you can see that the flood of foreign machines into the United States was really hurting the Motor Company. Unfortunately, worse was yet to come. (Note that these sales figures from Harley-Davidson's book *The Legend Begins* show sales of models ES and FS, which were not listed on the order blanks, and no sales for models ELS and FLS,

which were listed. The most probable explanation is that *Legend* was in error, and that the figures given for models ES and FS should have been for models ELS and FLS.)

The 1952 Hydra-Glides

For model year 1952, Harley-Davidson introduced a number of important changes, including the official introduction of the foot shift, oil screens for the tappet blocks, and revisions to the frame, muffler, and a number of other parts.

Models, Prices, and Option Groups
As was the case for 1951, only the high-compression models EL and FL were listed on the Harley-Davidson order blanks for 1952. Note, however, that the low-compression models E and F are listed in the Model Descriptions section of *The Legend Begins* as being available for 1952. Either *Legend* is in error, or these low-compression machines were special-order or export-only items.

When ordered with the optional foot shift, they were designated models ELF and FLF. When ordered with sidecar gearing (available only with hand shift, according to the order blank), they were designated models ELS and FLS. Despite the "ELF," "FLF," "ELS," and "FLS" designations, all 1952 Panheads engines were stamped 52EL or 52FL, followed in each case by the engine number. In other words, neither the "S" for "sidecar" nor the "F" for "foot shift" was stamped on the engine case.

Base-model 61s carried a retail price of $955, and base-model 74s carried a retail price of $970. These prices were misleading, however, because all new Panheads were shipped with one of two solo option groups or one police group for 1952, which added to the cost.

The Deluxe Solo Group sold for $73.50 and consisted of the following items:
- air cleaner
- 5.00x16-inch wheels and tires
- jiffy stand
- chrome rubber-mounted handlebars (either speedster or buckhorn)
- chrome front safety guard, rims, headlight, taillight, clutch cover, timer cover, primary-chain-inspection cover, muffler and exhaust-pipe covers
- stainless fork trim
- two "Deluxe OHV" name plates on fender, and
- polished fork sliders and brake side cover

Worth noting was that the Deluxe Solo Group was nearly $50 cheaper than in 1951, mostly because the saddlebags were deleted from the group.

The Utility Solo Group sold for $28.45 and included:
- black front safety guard

- air cleaner
- black wheels with 5.00x16-inch tires and
- jiffy stand

The Standard Police Group sold for $85.50 and included:

- black front safety guard
- jiffy stand
- black wheels with 5.00x16-inch tires
- air cleaner
- rear-wheel siren
- speedometer hand control and
- deluxe police solo saddle

Factory Paint Options

Five standard and three optional colors are listed as available for 1952. Standard at no extra charge were Brilliant Black, Persian Red, Rio Blue, Tropical Green, and Police Silver (for police bikes only). Optional for $10.30 extra were Metallic Bronco Bronze, Metallic Marine Blue, and White.

Chassis Updates and Detail Changes

The official introduction of foot shift and hand clutch were the biggest chassis updates for 1952, but Harley-Davidson also made several other changes, including revisions to the rear fender, frame, and mufflers, and the introduction of turn signals installed at the factory.

Foot Shift Until late 1951, when foot shift and hand clutch were quietly introduced, Harley riders could only look on in envy at all the Brit machines with foot shift, and the feature was seen as essential to a motorcycle's sporting image. Even Indian had beaten Harley when it fitted a few Chiefs with foot shift in late 1949 and early 1950.

Harley's management (and fan base) was as conservative then as it is now, so foot shift wasn't made mandatory. Instead, the foot-shift models ELF and FLF were listed as no-extra-cost options for 1952; hand shift was still available for those whom *The Enthusiast* of September 1951 called "[d]yed-in-the-wool hand shift riders." No reliable figures exist to tell us whether the new foot-shift models outsold the hand-shift models for 1952, but the figures listed in *The Legend Begins* show that by 1953, the foot-shift models were outselling the hand-shift models by a margin of nearly two to one. The margin continued to widen every year, and by 1965, only a few hand-shift models were produced.

Harley's foot-shift system used a hand lever on the left bar to operate the clutch and a foot lever at the front of the left footboard to change gears. (On most British and European machines, and even on Harley's Model K, the foot shifter was on the right.) The shift pattern is the now-familiar "one down, three up," with neutral between first and second. The hand lever for the front brake was moved to the right handlebar.

"Deluxe OHV" badges for the front fender were fitted on 1952–1954 Hydra-Glides ordered with the Deluxe Solo Group.

This bike has been dressed up with lots of chrome bits not fitted at the factory, including the dash, fender light, and chrome trim for the fender.

This machine is an FLF model, meaning it has a foot shift rather than a hand shift. Tanks for foot-shift machines were made without mountings for the shifter pivot and gate.

Many new components were added to the transmission on foot-shift models, including a redesigned shifter drum, an indexing cam, and a spring-loaded plunger to keep the transmission in the gear selected.

To help the weak human hand operate the stout Harley clutch, a spring-operated clutch "booster" was added; it mounted alongside the frame's left front down tube. Even with the booster, a manly squeeze was still required to pull in the clutch lever. The clutch-booster cover was painted black from 1952 to 1954, and cad plated thereafter. Chrome-plated covers were optional on new machines from 1959 on, although they were available through the accessory catalogs at an earlier date.

On foot-shift machines, a new left gas tank was fitted that was as smooth and streamlined as the right tank because the shifter-pivot lug and shifter gate were not needed with foot shift.

As mentioned earlier, the final F in "ELF" or "FLF" was not stamped into the left crankcase as part of the engine number, so there is no definitive way to tell whether a 1952 or later Panhead was originally hand shift or foot shift. Some of the parts provide strong clues—a left-hand gas tank without the shifter-pivot lug, for example—but

these parts may have been altered or retrofitted since the bike was built. Providing that the parts are available, the bike can be restored to either shift configuration and still be correct. That is, unless the bike is equipped with the optional three-speed transmission with reverse, which was only offered in hand-shift form. For 1952, the optional transmission was available for $8.60 at the time of order.

Frame The 1952 Panheads were fitted with another version of the wishbone frame. It was similar to the one introduced during the production run in 1951 (with rounded corners on the horn-block mounts), but it carried several new features: an inverted-U-shaped toolbox bracket with both legs of the U welded to the lower rear frame tube on the right side; a wider top motor mount (the mount was no longer L-shaped to match the L-shaped mounting hole); a wider combination rear-tank mount and seat T-bracket; a sturdier lower front engine mount; and the frame build date stamped on the right side of the top motor-mount bracket, just below where it was welded to the frame. This is a one-year-only frame; in 1953 the lower front motor mount was made even beefier.

Fenders A new rear fender was fitted for the third year in a row. The 1952 rear fender still had the single stainless-steel stripe on each side of the tail-light, but it had only one vertical channel stamped into the metal flat of the chain recess because the rest of the recess was now cut away. This style of fender was fitted through 1954.

On Panheads ordered with the Deluxe Solo Group, a 2-inch "Deluxe OHV" nameplate was fitted to each side of the front fender. Deluxe OHV nameplates are correct for all 1952–1954 Hydra-Glides ordered with the Deluxe group. Note, however, that these nameplates were not offered for sale separately from the group, so if a restored bike has these name plates, it should also have all the other items in the group. Hydra-Glide name plates were offered separately, for $1.50 a pair.

Turn Signals For 1952, front and rear turn signals were listed on the order blank for the first time. The lamps were essentially the same chromed, bullet-shaped lamps that were introduced as parking lights in 1949. The front signal lamps mount to the sides of the fork and have clear lenses. Rear signal lamps mount to the seat pan and also have clear lenses.

Factory turn-signal installations included a switch on the handlebar and an indicator light mounted to a plate attached to the handlebar riser link. Turn signals cost $16.75 when ordered on a new bike in 1952 or $15.75 when ordered separately from the accessory catalog.

Motor Updates
A number of small changes to the exhaust valves, oiling system, and charging system during model year 1952 added up to an even better Panhead motor.

Parko-Lubricized Exhaust Valves The most bizarre change was to "Parko-Lubricized" exhaust valves. The "Parko" part of the name was in honor of the Parkerizing process of applying a phosphate coating to the valves. The "Lubricized" part of the name was in honor of the coating's ability to absorb oil and hold it on the valves, keeping them well lubricated during the critical first miles of break-in.

Rotating Exhaust Valves Later in the 1952 production run, the introduction of "rotating" exhaust valves increased their reliability. Engine number 52FL3910 was the first to have these valves, which were fitted with a new valve-stem cap that kept the rocker arm from bearing directly on the top of the exhaust-valve stem, allowing the valve to be rotated by the swirling exhaust gases that are forced out the exhaust port.

The happy result of the valves rotating was that the valve seated in a slightly different position each time, so the tendency to "burn" exhaust valves was reduced. The rotating valves were used on FL models through 1960 and on FLH models through early 1958. Rotating exhaust valves were also available as a kit that could be retrofitted to earlier Panheads.

Low-Tone Muffler For 1952, the Mellow-Tone muffler was replaced by a new version called the "Low-Tone." Externally, the Low-Tone on the 1952 Panhead looked the same as the Mellow-Tone muffler that had been introduced in 1950, but it received extensive internal revision to give it an even mellower tone. The new design eschewed baffle plates for a resonating chamber and an expansion chamber, resulting in a muffler that was quieter and had less back pressure than the previous muffler. This muffler was supplied as the standard muffler on single-muffler systems through 1965.

Oil Pump Over hundreds of cycles of seating and unseating, the check balls in Panhead oil pumps would develop ridges. Balls being balls, sometimes they would roll slightly while open, so the worn-in ridge would not seat evenly against the stop. The result is that oil from the tank would drain into the crankcase when the bike was shut off—a problem known as "wet-sumping."

To remedy this problem, Harley engineers designed a new pump with stemmed check balls that would ensure more consistent seating of the ball. The pump was another of the running changes introduced during the 1952 production year. The oil pressure was no longer was adjustable on the new pump, and the new check valves proved to be only marginally more reliable than the old round check balls, so the pump was used only on late-1952 to early-1954 Panheads.

Tappet-Block Oil Screens About midway through the 1952 season, starting with engine number "about 52FL3529" (according to *Shop Dope* No. 330), a new right crankcase was introduced that was the same as the 1948 to early-1952 cases except that a boss for a screen and check valve was added to the case, just to the right of the rear tappet block.

Oil to the cylinder-head feed passages was routed into the boss and filtered through the screen, ensuring that the oil to the heads and hydraulic lifters was free of larger chunks of dirt and foreign particles. The check ball prevented the oil in the passage from draining back into the case after the motor was shut off, so that any lifters that collapse under spring pressure will quickly refill when the motor is started. The screen and

This style of fender bumper was optional for 1949–1954.

ball assembly were held in place by a straight-slotted cap screw that threads into the boss.

The screen proved useful in keeping dirt out of the lifters, but it had to be cleaned periodically or it would restrict oil flow to the rockers and lifters. The check ball was less effective, and was soon eliminated from production. In any case, the check ball was not needed after 1952 because in 1953 the hydraulic lifters were relocated to a new position, below the pushrods.

Straight-Slot Gear-Cover Screws As it had been for the 1948 and 1949 Panheads, the gear cover on the 1952 machines was once again fastened by straight-slot screws. Straight-slot gear-cover screws are correct for 1952–1965 Panheads.

Generators Early in the production year, the Model 32 three-brush generator (which had been used on all non-police Harley twins since 1932) was replaced by the Model 52 generator. The new generator was also a three-brush design that was used in conjunction with a cut-out relay (still mounted just forward of the ignition timer) instead of a voltage regulator to power the 6-volt charging system. The Model 52 generator was fitted to civilian Panheads through 1957.

Radio-equipped police bikes also got a new generator. In place of the two-brush Model 48 radio generator, the 1952 police bikes were fitted with the Model 52 radio generator. Like the generator it replaced, the Model 52 radio generator was a two-brush, 6-volt generator with an attached cooling fan and a separate voltage regulator. The new radio generator had a redesigned field coil and wider brushes, allowing it to produce more current (20 amps versus 18 amps) at a lower rpm than the older generator.

Options and Accessories

For those riders who demanded color coordination, the popular King Size saddlebags were offered with leather dyed Rio Blue, Persian Red, or Tropical Green for bikes ordered in these colors—and the cost for these leather beauties was only $1 more than for the plain black ones. They must not have been a popular option, though, because these bags were again offered in 1953—even though Rio Blue, Persian Red, and Tropical Green were not offered on new motorcycles. The black bags could be ordered with red or white trim, and even with white fringe.

Production for 1952

For 1952, Panhead sales dropped by nearly 20 percent. Only 6,700 Panheads went out the factory door, consisting of 5,554 FL, 186 FS, 918 EL, and 42 ES. Note that these sales figures from Harley-Davidson's book *The Legend Begins*, show sales of models ES and FS, which were not listed on the order blanks, and no sales for models ELS and FLS, which were listed on the blank. The most probable explanation is that *Legend* was in error, and that the figures for models ES and FS should have been for models ELS and FLS.

Sales of the venerable 61 models had dropped to fewer than one in five, so Harley-Davidson discontinued the model at the end of 1952.

The 1953 Hydra-Glides

For 1953, Harley-Davidson designers concentrated their energies on improving the engine, and their efforts paid off in an elegant solution to the problems with ticking lifters that plagued the design.

Models, Prices, and Option Groups

For 1953, the 74 was offered with the choice of two motors—the high-compression FL motor and the new FLE Traffic Combination motor (described below). Each motor was available with hand shift (FL or FLE) or foot shift (FLF or FLEF) and with optional police or sidecar gearing. Per usual Harley-Davidson practice, only FL or FLE, not the "F," is stamped into the case as part of the serial number.

Base-model machines carried a retail price of $1,000, a modest $30 increase over the previous year's prices for the FL. These prices were misleading, however, because all new Panheads were shipped with one of two solo option groups or one police group for 1953, which added to the cost.

The Deluxe Solo Group sold for $83.30 and consisted of the following items:
- chrome front safety guard, rims, headlight, taillight, clutch cover, timer cover, inspection cover, muffler, and exhaust-pipe covers

- air cleaner
- 5.00x16-inch wheels and tires
- jiffy stand
- chrome rubber-mounted speedster or buck-horn handlebars
- oil-filter assembly
- stainless-steel fork trim
- 2-inch Deluxe OHV name plates on front fender
- polished fork sliders and brake side cover
The Standard Solo Group sold for $28.45 and included:
- black front safety guard
- air cleaner
- black wheels with 5.00x16-inch tires
- jiffy stand
- speedster or buckhorn handlebars
The Standard Police Group sold for $85.50 and included:
- black front safety guard
- jiffy stand
- black wheels with 5.00x16-inch tires
- air cleaner
- rear-wheel siren

- speedometer hand control
- deluxe police solo saddle
- speedster or buckhorn handlebars

Factory Paint Options
For 1953, Hydra-Glides were again available in five standard and three optional colors. Standard at no extra charge were Brilliant Black, Pepper Red, Glacier Blue, Forest Green, and Police

Top: For 1953, Harley continued the basic Hydra-Glide style set in 1951.

Bottom: The two-piece tank badges were used through 1953.

The big functional change for 1953 was a redesign of the valve train that relocated the hydraulic lifters from atop the pushrods to below them.

The seat shown is styled like the later Super Deluxe Buddy Seat.

Silver (for police bikes only). Optional for $10.30 extra were Cavalier Brown, Glamour Green, and White.

Chassis Updates and Detail Changes

Chassis updates for 1953 were few and minor. The frame for 1953 was basically the same as for 1952, except that the lower front motor mount was beefed up. This frame was the last frame fitted

with horn-mount blocks, because a new horn would be introduced in 1954. The optional Deluxe Buddy Seat was covered in vinyl (instead of leather) for 1953 and later.

Speedometer The Panhead speedometer was due for a facelift after five years of production, so it got one for 1953. The 1953-style Stewart-Warner speedometer differs from the 1948–1952 speedometer in many small details: the raised ring that forms the background for the numbers is now painted black (instead of greenish gray); the lower face is painted dark gray (instead of bluish gray); the numbers span 1 through 12 (instead of 10 through 120) in a larger block type, and the 2-mile-per-hour division marks, with longer and wider marks denoting the 10s, are painted on the underside of the glass (instead of being painted on the center section); the bar-and-shield emblem on the glass is replaced by "Harley-Davidson" in yellow-silver; the 1953 odometer and trip-meter-mile numerals are white on a black background (instead of black on a white background), and the tenth numerals are black (instead of red) on a white background; the pointer is white (instead of red); and the color of the painted numbers, mile-per-hour divisions, and words on the glass is now yellow-silver (instead of cream-ivory). This speedometer was used only for 1953 (the pointer was changed to red and the tenth numerals are red painted on a black background for 1954).

Motor Updates

The Panhead engine was significantly updated and improved for 1953, with a redesign of the hydraulic-lifter and oil-return systems and the introduction of a new low-performance version of the Model F motor to replace the discontinued Model E motor.

Relocated Hydraulic Lifters After many updates to the oil pumps, lifters, and rocker arms implemented from 1948 to 1952 that never really solved the Panhead motor's chronic problems with ticking lifters, Harley-Davidson designers got serious for 1953 and relocated the lifters from their former position atop the pushrods to their new location at the top of the tappets, below the pushrods. The new lifters were far closer to the oil pump, so the oil pressure to them was more constant and reliable.

Many new parts were required to implement the new system: right crankcase, tappet blocks, tappets, lifters, adjusters, and pushrods. To supply oil to the new lifter location, the new case had an oil passage to feed oil to the tappet blocks, the new tappet blocks (now made of cast iron) had a passage to carry oil from the case to a hole in the tappet, and the new tappets had a hole in the flat

A new version of the motor was offered for 1953: the FLE Traffic Combination, which was the basic FL motor fitted with the milder cam and smaller carb from the discontinued EL models. These modifications were meant to make the engine more docile for traffic control and escort use.

The accessory fender lamp gives the 1950s' version of a space-age look to the front of this 1953 Hydra-Glide.

on its side to pick up oil from the tappet block and feed it to the lifter, which was slip-fit into a hole in the top of the tappet. The new pushrod had the ball end at the top rather than at the bottom, a pressed-in bottom fitting that was threaded for the screw-in adjuster and was 9¼ inches long (not including the adjuster). The new lifter system worked so well that it was used through the end of the Panhead line with only a few minor changes to the pushrods and adjusters.

Like all tappet blocks from 1950 to 1952, early-1953 tappet blocks were secured with eight straight-slot or Phillips-head screws (there was no real pattern as to which motors were fitted with which type). Later, 1953 tappet blocks were secured by eight hex-head screws without lock washers, and these hex screws were used through 1965.

Return Oiling System In pre-1953 motors, oil from the heads was returned through a passage in the left side of each cylinder to passages in the left and right crankcases, where it drained into the cases. In the 1953 motor, oil from the heads drained down a passage in the left side of the cylinder and through a hole in the cylinder wall, where it helped lubricate the cylinders and contributed to the splash lubrication of the other bottom-end components.

To help keep the extra oil out of the combustion chamber, new oil-control rings were introduced. These rings were made of heat-treated steel that conformed to the cylinder walls better than the old cast-iron rings. The new oil return used redesigned left and right crankcases and new cylinders. The new left case was the same as the 1952 case, except the oil channel on the rear-cylinder base and the oil passage on the front-cylinder base were omitted. The new right case was the same as the late 1952 case, except the oil channel on the rear-cylinder base was omitted. The new cylinders each had a smaller rocker-feed passage on the right side and a new-style oil-return passage leading to a hole in the cylinder wall. These new crankcases were used on 1953 and 1954 models, and the new cylinders were used through 1962.

The FLE Traffic Combination Motor The 61-cubic-inch Model EL had been discontinued at the end of the 1953 season. But the 61 had qualities that endeared it to police departments and commercial users. Its smaller carb and milder camshaft made it ideal for escort work and use in heavy traffic. To compensate these users for the loss of their beloved 61s, Harley-Davidson introduced a special FLE Traffic Combination version of the 74 that was fitted with the cam and M-61 Linkert carburetor from the 61 to give the Traffic Combination 74 the excellent low-speed performance of the 61.

The Traffic Combination motor was offered from 1953 to 1956. It stayed as introduced for model years 1953 and 1954, but for model years 1955 and 1956, it was fitted with the standard 74's M-74B carburetor.

Other Changes In late 1953, a new pinion-shaft bearing was introduced that had 24½×0.270-inch rollers instead of 12½×0.600-inch rollers. The new bearing used the same spacers as the old bearing.

Production for 1953
The foot-shift option proved very popular again for 1953, outselling the hand shift by nearly two to one. Unfortunately, the new feature wasn't bringing in the new customers that Harley-Davidson had hoped it would, and sales eroded by another 20 percent. Total sales of 5,337 Hydra-Glides (1,986 with hand shift and 3,351 with foot shift) were fewer than the number of FL models (let alone the EL models) sold the previous year. The number of FLEs sold wasn't recorded. This was also the year that Harley's long-time rival, Indian, closed its factory doors forever. At the end of its 50th year, Harley-Davidson's prospects for the future looked very grim.

The 1954 Hydra-Glides

In September of 1953, as the 1954 models were being built, Harley celebrated its 50th Anniversary, so the 1954 models were designated Anniversary models. This may seem odd to us today, given that Harley-Davidson celebrated its 90th Anniversary in 1993 and is planning on celebrating its 100th anniversary in 2003. Nevertheless, that's what the company did, and all the 1954 models, including the Hydra-Glides, were billed as 50th Anniversary models.

Models, Prices, and Option Groups
The 50th Anniversary Hydra-Glides were offered in standard FL and optional FLE Traffic Combination form. Each motor was available with hand shift (designated Model FL or FLE) or foot shift (designated Model FLF or FLEF). Per usual Harley-Davidson practice, only FL or FLE, not the "F" for "foot shift," is stamped into the case as part of the serial number. Police or sidecar gearing was also available as a no-cost option.

Base-model machines carried a retail price of $1,015, a modest $15 increase over the previous year's prices. Also per usual Harley-Davidson practice, these prices were misleading, because all new 1954 Hydra-Glides were shipped with one of two solo option groups or one police group, which added to the cost.

The Deluxe Solo Group consisted of the following items:
- chrome front safety guard, rims, headlight, taillight, clutch inspection cover, timer cover, primary-chain-inspection cover, muffler, and exhaust-pipe covers
- air cleaner
- 5.00x16-inch tires
- jiffy stand
- chrome rubber-mounted handlebars (speedster or buckhorn)
- oil-filter assembly
- stainless fork trim
- chrome-plated horn and cover
- 2-inch Deluxe OHV nameplates on fender
- polished fork sliders and brake side cover

The Standard Solo Group included:
- black front safety guard
- air cleaner
- black wheels with 5.00x16-inch tires
- jiffy stand
- choice of speedster or buckhorn handlebars

The Standard Police Group included:
- black front safety guard
- jiffy stand
- black wheels with 5.00x16-inch tires
- air cleaner
- rear-wheel siren
- speedometer hand control
- police deluxe solo saddle
- choice of speedster or buckhorn handlebars

Factory Paint Options
The Panheads were offered in eight standard, single-color paint schemes and seven optional two-tone schemes (no extra charge) for 1954: Pepper Red, Glacier Blue, Forest Green, Daytona Ivory, Anniversary Yellow, Black, Silver (Police Group only), White (Police Group only), Pepper Red tanks with Daytona Ivory fenders, Glacier Blue tanks with Daytona Ivory fenders, Forest Green tanks with Daytona Ivory fenders, Daytona Ivory tanks with Pepper Red fenders, Daytona Ivory tanks with Glacier Blue fenders, Daytona Ivory tanks with Forest Green fenders, and for Motor Maids members only, Cadillac Grey tanks and Azure Blue fenders.

Chassis Updates
Chassis on the 50th Anniversary Hydra-Glides benefited from many subtle changes, including a new frame, new tank badges, a handsome new horn, revised hand controls, and other updates.

Fiftieth Anniversary Medallion In celebration of the company's golden anniversary, all 1954 Hydra-Glides were fitted with a fiftieth anniversary medallion on the top of the front fender. The medallion was a gold-satin-finished, stamped badge consisting of a 2½-inch disc background with a large V superimposed over the disc and a

Harley-Davidson celebrated its fiftieth anniversary in the fall of 1953, so its 1954 models were designated as Anniversary models. The one shown here is painted in the special Anniversary Yellow offered that year. It was restored by Elmer Ehnes.

To commemorate the anniversary, Harley fitted the Hydra-Glides with a spiffy new medallion on the front fender. These were a standard item, so no 1954 restoration is complete without one. This view also shows the front fender tip that was standard from 1949 to 1956.

Anniversary Hydra-Glides were also fitted with new control spirals that were held in place by a screw threaded into the ends of the new handlebar.

Three different frames were used during 1954 production. This machine is fitted with the wishbone style of frame, of which there were two versions for 1954. In late 1954, a new straight-leg frame was introduced and was used through 1955.

bar and shield superimposed over the V. "Harley-Davidson" appears in script on the bar, "50 Years" on the top part of the shield, and "American Made" on the lower part of the shield. This lovely medallion is hard to find today, but no restoration of a 1954 Panhead is complete without it.

Revised Tank Badges Perhaps the most noticeable change for 1954 was to the gas-tank emblem. Basically, it was the same as the 1951–1953 type, except that the chrome underline strip was omitted. This emblem was used for 1954 only.

Frames With the introduction of a new horn mounted on the engine, the horn-mount blocks were no longer welded to the wishbone frame down tubes. Even so, the very first 1954 frames still had down tubes flattened in the area where the horn mounts would have been welded. Mid-production 1954 frames were still of the wishbone design, but the down tubes were no longer flattened.

Late in 1954 a new frame was introduced—in a sense, reintroduced. The wishbone style of frame that had been introduced on the first Panheads in 1948 was replaced by a new straight-leg style of frame, similar to the one used on the last of the Knuckleheads in 1947. The frame change is most discernible when the bike is viewed from the front. The down tubes of the wishbone frame dogleg out noticeably to each side; the down tubes of the straight-leg frame are straight tubes. This new frame was also used for 1955.

Safety guards for the 1954 wishbone frames were the same as the guards used since 1951. Late-1954 straight-leg frames once again used the 1941–1947 guard. This was a one-piece tubular guard with an inverted-T-shaped mounting bracket (with four holes) held to the frame by two U-bolts. It was used from late 1954 through 1957. Standard guards were painted black, but chrome-plated guards were optional for $6 at the time of order or as part of the Deluxe Solo Group.

Jubilee Trumpet Horn The second most noticeable change for 1954 was the lovely new Jubilee trumpet horn. Supplying the honk was a new horn body mounted on the left side of the motor. Delivering the honk was a long trumpet tube that wound between the cylinders to the right side of the motor and bent 90 degrees forward before fluting out into a graceful trumpet. It was an instant classic.

Trumpets were cadmium- or chrome-plated steel (sometimes listed as "polished" on the order blanks). The horn cover was listed as chrome plated for 1954 and 1955, but was listed as polished for later years. The horn bodies were painted black. An instant classic, the Jubilee horn was fitted to Panheads through the 1964 season.

Handlebars and Controls New, "faster-acting" throttle and spark-control spirals were also introduced for 1954. These were held to the handlebars by a ⅜-inch end screw that threaded onto the end of the handlebar, much like the 1948 spirals had. To accommodate the new spirals, revised handlebars with threaded ends were introduced. These handlebars were otherwise the same as the 1951–1953 bars, and were offered in Buckhorn or Speedster lengths. Solid-mounted bars were black; optional rubber-mounted bars were chromed.

Speedometer For the second year in a row, the speedometer was given a facelift. The 1954 Stewart-Warner speedometer was the same as the 1953 one, except that the pointer was red and the tenth-mile numerals were painted red on a black background. This speedometer was a one-year-only item.

Brakes In an attempt to prevent brake squeal and chatter, engineers shortened the brake linings for 1954, which resulted in smoother, quieter, more powerful brakes. These shoes and linings were still being fitted to the last Panheads in 1965.

Shifter Shaft A new-style shifter shaft was fitted in 1954. It was no longer splined, so a new foot lever and optional heel lever were also introduced to mount on the new, smooth shaft.

Motor Updates
Model year 1954 was also a year of many minor updates to the engine to make it quieter and more reliable.

Four-Rib Gear Cover A new style of gear cover made its debut in 1954. Previous Panhead gear covers (and most of the Knucklehead covers, too) had featured eight horizontal ribs, but the new cover had only four ribs. The gear cover was still sand-cast, but now had the number 25217-40 cast in relief on the inner side. It was also fitted with a new bushing for the new pinion shaft that was

The "Deluxe OHV" nameplates shown on this fender were included in the Deluxe Solo package.

This bike was fitted with the FLE motor, which had been introduced as a low-performance engine for police use in 1953.

The stripes alongside the taillight were back for 1954, but they were discontinued at the end of the year.

The business end of the new-for-1954 Jubilee trumpet horn.

This badge was fitted to the front fender of all Hydra-Glides for 1954.

This speedometer was used for 1954 only. It is like the 1953 speedometer, differing only in that the pointer was painted red, and the tenth-mile numerals were painted red on a black background.

also introduced for 1954. This style of four-rib gear cover is correct for 1954–1957 motors.

Shafts and Gears The pinion shaft, oil-pump worm gear, and pinion gear were redesigned for 1954 to reduce noise from the gear case. Gone were the splines for the pinion gear, replaced by a taper and key. A key was also used to hold the worm gear in place. This new pinion shaft was used only for 1954. A new oil pump was fitted that contained many internal revisions, including a change back to round check balls, replacing the stemmed check balls used since late 1952. This new oil pump was used through 1955.

During the 1954 production run (starting with motor number 54FLE2077), two lock screws were added to prevent the race for the pinion-shaft bearing from turning in the case. A new race, having two seating notches for the lock screws, was introduced and the holes were drilled and tapped in the cases to the notch positions. Subsequent orders for replacement races to be installed in earlier motors were supplied with notched races, and *Shop Dope* No. 348A recommends that these earlier cases be drilled for the lock screws with a new Harley-Davidson drilling jig.

Later in 1954, a new bearing was introduced (starting with engine number 54FL5010). This bearing was wider overall, eliminating the bearing spacer previously used on the flywheel side. The new bearing still used 24 rollers, but the rollers were longer (0.360 inch vs. 0.270 inch) to increase the bearing area.

Aluminum D-Rings Very late in 1954, new-style D-rings were introduced. These rings were cast of aluminum and were made much thicker than the old-style welded-steel D-rings to help seal the rocker covers more efficiently. Instead of 12 mounting-screw holes, only six were drilled in the new D-ring.

The new rings were much more rigid than the old D-rings, so Harley-Davidson engineers thought that six hex-head cap screws would be enough to seal the rocker cover. Unfortunately, they were wrong. The covers often leaked, so revised D-rings with 12 mounting holes were issued for 1956.

Options and Accessories
With new options such as plastic hard bags and dual exhaust, along with restyled leather bags, seats, and fender bumpers, Harley-Davidson put a lot of effort into updating the look of its accessories for model year 1954.

The centerpiece of that update was comets. Harley-Davidson must have gotten a hell of a deal on winged nickel comets in 1954, because the engineers put them everywhere they would fit, as we'll see.

Royalite Saddlebags Plastic saddlebags were first offered by Harley-Davidson as an option for the Hydra-Glide in 1954. These bags were black Royalite bags trimmed with two of those silver comets, along with seven silver dots arranged in a reverse-L-shape in front of the comets. These hard bags were available on 1954–1956 Panheads. (White bags were not offered on the order sheets until 1959, but white Royalite bags were later offered as a retrofit kit.)

Harley's new plastic bags were far more weatherproof than their leather counterparts and much easier to remove, too. Pull two pins and each bag lifts free of its frame. Opinion varies on their styling, however. Some riders think they look great; others prefer the classic look of leather bags. Once again, however, Harley-Davidson was smart enough to accommodate both points of view on its order blanks.

Restyled Buddy Seats The restyled Deluxe Buddy seat for 1954 featured 2 inches of foam padding, plastic covering, and a new skirt with—you guessed it—comets, one on each side. It could be ordered for $23.75 (exchange) on a new bike. For those of really tender tush, a Super Deluxe Buddy Seat was offered. It featured 4 inches of foam padding, leather covering, and, of course, the comets. It could be ordered for $35 (exchange) on a new bike.

Restyled Leather Bags Two sizes of leather bags were still offered for 1954, and both were restyled in the 1954 comet theme. The large leather Speed King bags cost $37.75 at the time of order. Speed King saddlebags for 1954–1956 were decorated with white piping (around the edge of the top, along the lower edge of the cover, and along the edge of the side), nine rectangular nickel pieces arranged in three rows of three (angling toward the rear) on the top of the cover, two nickel comet pieces on the sides of the cover, three leather straps angling toward the back with angled chrome speed buckles, and three round nickel dots near the lower edge of the side (one just to the front of each buckle). A fringed version of the Speed King was also offered, for $39.95.

The smaller Streamliner bags were restyled with white piping, three rows of square nickel spots on the top of the cover, and the slanted "speed buckles" (except that there are only two, rather than three). In addition, these bags now had four large nickel dots around the sides of the cover, a slanted row of nickel dots ahead of the front buckle, three slanted rows of dots between the two buckles, and a slanted row of dots behind the rear buckle. This style of bags is correct for 1954–1956 and sold for $28.50.

Dual Exhaust Though not listed on the order blanks until 1956, and thus not really "correct" for

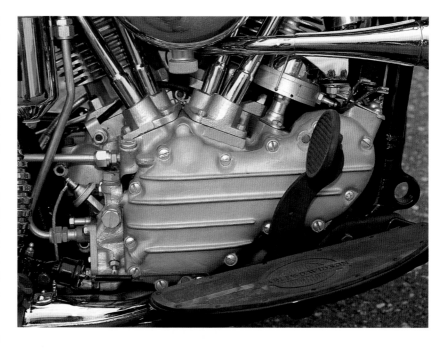

This view shows the new gear cover with four cooling fins, rather than eight, which was introduced in 1954 and was standard through 1962.

For 1954, Harley reused the "Harley-Davidson" tank badges but omitted the underline bars. By this time, the hand-shift FLs and FLEs were outsold by the foot-shift FLF and FLEF models.

Serial numbers were tamped on a pad on the left crankcase during the Panhead years.

1954 was the last year for styling cues such as the stripe on the rear fender and the tank badges, which had begun in 1951.

a restoration of a 1954 Panhead, a dual-exhaust system was first offered for the Hydra-Glides in the 1954 accessory catalog. The dual-exhaust system used the same front header pipe and S-pipe as the single system and kept two of the mufflers used on the single system, but the other pipes were unique to the dual system. The front cylinder was connected exclusively to the right muffler through the front header, the S-pipe, and a new, straight pipe. The rear cylinder connected exclusively to the left cylinder through a new pipe that snaked back and to the left from the exhaust port. The new left and right pipes were chrome plated.

Fender Bumpers Two styles of optional rear bumper were offered for 1954 and 1955. The old-style bumper (available since late 1948) featured a chromed, tubular bumper that gently curved in at the ends. The new bumper featured a larger, chrome bumper piece and could be ordered with the "bologna-slicer" grille. Either bumper could be ordered for $9.75, and the grille cost an additional $6.90. Neither of these bumpers was sturdy enough to offer any real protection. They were just another means of hanging more chrome on a Panhead.

Production for 1954

Even the anniversary models didn't arrest the slump in sales. Panhead sales finally bottomed out (temporarily) in 1954, at 4,757 units, just over one-third of what they had been in 1948. Power and performance of the FL had not improved appreciably since 1948, while the competing British bikes were getting bigger and faster each year. Customers wanted more horsepower, and Harley decided to give it to them.

The 1955 Hydra-Glides

After years of minor updates, Harley-Davidson made major changes for 1955. Most important, the company beefed up the Panhead lower end so it was ready for further power increases. Good thing, too, because in mid-year Harley released the hot-rod Model FLH Super Sport. More noticeable, and just as important, the Hydra-Glide chassis was also updated for a more modern look.

Models, Prices, and Option Groups

At the beginning of the model year, the Hydra-Glide was offered in FL and FLE (which now had only the cam from the old Model EL, but not its smaller carburetor). Later in the year, the FLH Super Sport made its debut. Each motor was available with hand shift (designated Model FL, FLE, or FLH) or foot shift (designated Model FLF, FLEF, or FLHF). Per usual Harley-Davidson practice, only the letters FL, FLE, or FLH (not the "F" for "foot shift") were stamped into the case as part of the serial number. Police or sidecar gearing was also available as a no-cost option.

Base-model FLs and FLEs retailed for $1,015 (same as the previous year), but base-model FLHs retailed for $1,083. Also per usual Harley-Davidson practice, these prices were misleading, because all new Panheads were shipped with one of two solo option groups, one sidecar group, or one police group for 1955, which added to the cost.

The Deluxe Solo Group sold for $88 and consisted of the following items:
- chrome front safety guard
- air cleaner
- 5.00x16-inch wheels and tires
- jiffy stand
- chrome rubber-mounted handlebars (speedster or buckhorn)
- chrome rims, headlight, clutch inspection cover, timer cover, primary-chain-inspection cover, muffler, and exhaust-pipe covers
- oil-filter assembly
- stainless fork trim
- polished fork sliders and brake side cover
- chrome-plated horn and cover
- front-fender medallion

The Standard Solo Group sold for $31.50 and included:
- black front safety guard
- air cleaner
- black wheels with 5.00x16-inch tires
- jiffy stand
- choice of speedster or buckhorn handlebars

The Deluxe Sidecar Group sold for $129 and included:
- windshield and apron
- spare wheel and carrier
- 5.00x16-inch wheels and tires
- sidecar lamp and wiring
- two chrome rims

In addition, Harley-Davidson recommended that all motorcycles ordered for sidecar use be equipped with the optional changeable-trail fork, for $7.

The Standard Police Group sold for $90 and included:
- black front safety guard
- jiffy stand
- 5.00x16-inch wheels and tires
- air cleaner
- rear-wheel siren
- speedometer hand control

Hydra-Glides were substantially updated and restyled for 1955. This beauty was restored by John Villjoen and Scott Lange.

Among the new bits was another front-fender badge, shown here.

- deluxe solo saddle
- front-fender medallion

Factory Paint Options
Seven standard colors and one optional color were offered for single-color schemes. Standard were the following: Pepper Red, Atomic Blue, Anniversary Yellow, Aztec Brown, Black, Silver

The most substantial change was from roller bearings to Timken bearings in the lower end.

This style of tank badge was fitted for 1955 and 1956.

(Police Group only), and White (Police Group only). A special Hollywood Green paint option was available for $10 extra. On this option, the outer chain guard, toolbox, battery cover, and oil tank were painted in Hollywood Green.

If the buyer wanted a two-color scheme, many combinations were available for 1955. The order blank offered the following: "Any combination of tanks in one color and fenders in another using our standard colors, except Hollywood Green, will be supplied at no extra charge."

Chassis Updates and Detail Changes

On the 1955 Hydra-Glides, Harley-Davidson restyled many key parts to give the old Big Twin a front-to-back facelift. Restyled for the year were the front-fender medallion, fork tins, tank emblems, and taillight.

Front-Fender Medallion Replacing the 50th Anniversary medallion of 1954 on the front fender was a new V-shaped medallion for 1955. These medallions were included with the Deluxe Solo or Standard Police groups (but not with the Standard Solo Group), and may have been available separately.

The medallion included a large V with a bar and shield superimposed. The words "Harley-Davidson" were stamped out in relief on the bar. The year "1955" was stamped in relief on the top part of the shield, and the model designation "FL" or "FLH" was stamped on the bottom part of the shield. These medallions were fitted only to 1955 bikes. (FL medallions should only be fitted to bikes with motors stamped FL or FLE, and FLH medallions should only be fitted to bikes with motors stamped FLH.)

"V" Fork Tins and Rubber-Mounted Headlight At the front, new upper fork covers updated the look. The four horizontal stripes on each side of the headlight were replaced by three diagonal stripes on each side, cradling the headlight in a V shape. Like the previous cover, this cover was black-painted steel unless the optional stainless-steel fork trim ($10.65 additional) or Deluxe Solo Group was specified at the time of order.

Also new for the year, the headlight was rubber-mounted to reduce breakage of headlight mounts and mounting bolts, as well as to insulate the lamp filaments from engine and road vibration. As before, the headlight bucket was painted black unless the bike was ordered with the Deluxe Solo Group or the optional chrome headlight. The new fork cover and rubber-mounted headlight were fitted to Panheads through 1959.

Tank Emblems Replacing the "Harley-Davidson" script tank emblems of 1954 were massive new tank emblems for 1955. The new tank emblems were large castings with "Harley-Davidson" in script, superimposed on a large V, which was superimposed on a large swoosh. These emblems were as ornate and complex as the 1954 emblems were spare. They were fitted to Hydra-Glides for 1955 and 1956.

Taillight At the rear, the die-cast, tombstone-shaped taillight with integral license-plate bracket used since 1948 was replaced by an oval-shaped, stamped-steel taillight and a separate license-plate bracket mounted ahead of the light. In *The Enthusiast* of September 1954, Harley-Davidson claims a weight reduction of 15 ounces for the new light.

Taillight bodies were painted the color of the fender, but the rim piece that frames the lens was chrome plated. This style of taillight was fitted to the Big Twins through 1972. The license-plate bracket was adjustable and painted black (standard) or chrome plated. The new taillight and license bracket required a new rear fender with the necessary mounting holes. The fender and bracket were used through 1957.

Speedometer The 1955 Stewart-Warner speedometer was slightly changed from the 1954 speedometer: the tenth-mile numerals were painted black on a white background (instead of red numerals on a black background). This speedometer was used only for 1955.

Clutch-Booster Covers Instead of being painted black, the clutch-booster covers of standard 1955 Hydra-Glides were cadmium plated. Standard

The heads and intake manifold were also redesigned for better sealing.

Also new for 1955 was the taillight. Its body was painted the same color as the fender for 1955-1965 Panheads, but it was fitted with the chrome lens door shown.

clutch-booster covers were cad plated through the end of the Panhead line, but chrome covers were available through the accessory catalogs. Chrome booster covers were first offered on new Panheads in 1959, as part of the Chrome Finish Group and separately.

(chrome covers were first offered on order blanks in 1959).

Motor Updates

Early Panhead motors were essentially the new top end atop the old Knucklehead bottom end. With the Panhead top end came more power, and further updates increased it to the point that the old Knuckle bottom end could barely keep up and was probably too weak for further power increases, so the company finally got around to beefing up the bottom end for 1955. At the same time, the company reworked the intake tract to make it less leaky and modernized the exterior of the engine, too, before taking advantage of the stronger bottom end to create a new hot-rod.

Timken Bearings and Compensating Sprocket

The bottom end was beefed up by redesigning the left crankcase and sprocket shaft to use tapered Timken bearings in place of the former roller bearings. The new sprocket shaft was keyed only at the flywheel end, had 10 splines at the sprocket end, and was made of harder, 4620 nickel-moly steel. At $4\frac{15}{16}$ inches long and $1\frac{1}{4}$ inches in diameter, the new shaft was both longer and larger in diameter than the previous sprocket shaft (which had been used in all Harley Big Twins since 1930). This new sprocket shaft was used for 1955 only.

The new left case featured a smooth surface inside the primary-chain mounting ring (previously, there had been a raised mounting boss and three radial ribs) and the number "24599-55" cast in relief on the inside of the case. This redesigned case was used through 1957.

Timken bearings are designed to take thrust and radial loads, so the flywheels were also redesigned for use without thrust washers. The left flywheel was a one-year-only part that had a thick shoulder for the Timken bearing to seat against.

The pinion-shaft bearing was also replaced with one of larger area, so the right crankcase and pinion shaft were redesigned to accommodate the new bearing. The new shaft was "crowned" to reduce end pressure on the bearing rollers. Like the new left case, the new right case and gear shaft were used through 1957.

O-Ring Manifolds and New Heads

Like the Knuckle before it, the Panhead engine made use of "plumber nuts" at the intake-manifold junctions. These manifolds were simple, and sealed fairly well when new, but the solid joint they created between the heads and the carburetor transmitted and amplified the effects of the engine's vibration, foaming the gasoline in the carburetor float bowls. Over time, vibration also caused the manifold bushings to wear against the manifold and create air leaks. Even when they sealed well, the plumber

This 1955 was equipped with the accessory aluminum cooling ring for the front brake and the new "venetian blind" fender bumper.

For 1955, three stripes on each side of the headlight formed a pleasing chevron shape.

Other Changes Horn mounting brackets were strengthened. Rear fenders were stripped of the single stainless-steel stripe that had been fitted alongside the taillight. Finally, a new wing-bolt closure (in place of a lock) was fitted to the toolbox. Toolboxes were still painted black

nuts were a pain to properly loosen or tighten in the cramped V of the motor.

For 1955, Harley-Davidson released a completely new manifold design (with new cylinder heads to match) that eliminated all these problems: the O-ring manifold. No longer was the intake manifold fastened to the inlet nipple with the large plumber nuts. Instead, a large O-ring was sandwiched between the end of each nipple and the end of each manifold tube, and each junction was covered and sealed by a large strap clamp. A lip on each cylinder end of the T-shaped manifold helped hold the O-ring in place. The new iron manifold bore the cast-in number "27027-55," and was painted silver. This manifold was used through 1957.

The new cylinder heads were redesigned to include a cast-in inlet nipple (previous nipples had been separate steel pieces that threaded into the intake ports) that was designed to connect with the new O-ring intake manifold. Each head had the mark "16704 55 FRONT" or "16705 55 REAR" cast in relief on its underside between the pushrod holes.

Heads for 1955 were drilled for only six valve-cover mounting holes (rather than 12) because the ¾-inch aluminum D-rings with six holes (which had been introduced on very-late 1954

Panheads) were again used. (Note: Because the six-hole D-rings did not seal well, most 1955 Panheads were retrofitted with the later 12-hole D-rings and had the additional holes drilled into the heads for the mounting screws. Nevertheless, to be stock and original, 1955 Panheads should have the six-hole D-rings.)

Primary Cover Modernizing the look of the motor for 1955 was a new outer primary-chain cover. Instead of being angular and embossed with the "diamond" pattern of previous years, the new primary cover was rounded and smooth, and painted gloss black. It was fitted with a small

A smooth primary cover replaced the old "diamond" cover for 1954.

The 1955 speedometer was like the 1954 version, except that the tenth-mile numerals were changed to black on a white background.

Above: If you look closely under the tank, you can see the connectors for the new-style intake manifolds for 1955. Those connectors cover the o-rings that seal the junctions. Right and below right: The optional hard and soft saddlebags for 1955. Both styles of bags were first offered in 1954.

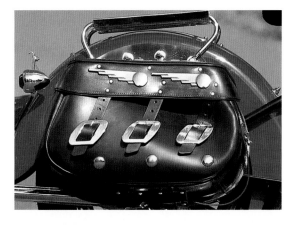

Below: This style of Deluxe Buddy Seat is correct for 1955. It was also introduced in 1954.

primary-chain-inspection cover and a larger clutch-inspection cover, and featured a raised strip running from the front edge to the clutch "bulge." The inspection covers were also painted black, with chrome-plated covers optional.

In addition, the new primary cover may have included a third cover, smaller and farther forward than the other two. I say "may have" because the hole that the cover plugs was added only if the motorcycle was ordered with the new, optional compensating sprocket (which acted as an engine shock absorber and sold for $15, exchange). This new cover allowed access to lubricate the compensating sprocket, was about the size of a quarter, and was chrome plated. The smooth primary cover was used through 1964.

The inner primary-chain cover was new as well, and was made in separate designs for foot- and hand-shift bikes. The main change is that the new cover had a larger sprocket-shaft hole and a revised mounting perch to bolt up to the revised left crankcase. The inner chain guard was mounted to the crankcase by three bolts with spring washers, and a gasket was fitted between the chain cover and crankcase. Spring washers and gaskets worked together to reduce rattling and vibration. These new inner primary covers were used through 1957.

The FLH Super Sport

During the 1955 production year, a hot-rodded version of the Hydra-Glide was introduced: the FLH. This machine featured a special motor with higher compression pistons and polished and flowed intake tracts that increased horsepower by about 10 percent. Since the normal "high-compression" FL was called the "Sport Solo," the higher-compression FLH was dubbed "Super Sport."

First-year FLHs were not fitted with any readily visible insignia of their hot-rod rank. In fact, the only way you could tell was to look for the FLH prefix on the serial-number stamping. They are only distinguishable from FL models by the "FLH" stamped into the motor as part of the serial number). Later FLHs (possibly including very late 1955 FLHs) were fitted with a special FLH decal on both sides of the oil tank.

Options and Accessories

Many of the accessories were restyled to go with the updated looks of the 1955 Panheads.

Seats Starting in 1955, Harley-Davidson standard solo seats were stitched with the same type of rolled seam used on 1950 and later Deluxe Solo Seats (see the description in that section). This style of seat was standard through 1965.

The optional Deluxe Solo Seat (which could be ordered in place of the standard saddle for

$7.40) was restyled for 1955. Instead of a three-piece leather skirt with plastic rosettes, the new saddle had a one-piece Royalite rubber skirt with a wing-shaped lobe at the each side, each lobe decorated with a nickel piece shaped like an elongated diamond. The shorter rear part of the skirt was decorated with seven nickel rectangles. As promised in *The Enthusiast* of September 1954, the new seat was a "big hit with pleasure riders and police officers." This flashy new saddle was a correct option for 1955–1965 Panheads.

Front-Fender Bumper A new-style, optional front bumper was introduced in late 1955. Depending on who is asked, this bumper is called the "bologna slicer," "antenna," or "Venetian blind" bumper because it had three chrome "blades" with their edges pointed forward (the blades were similar to those included in the optional grille for the rear bumper). The blades bridged the gap between two chromed, J-shaped tubes that mounted to the fender and reached forward and up, each topped off with a chromed ball. This bumper offered little in the way of protection, but gave a very 1950s look to the front end. The bumper was an $8.75 option in 1955. This bumper was a correct option for 1955–57 Panheads.

Sidecar Changes With the introduction of the new taillight and license-plate bracket, these elements were eliminated on the sidecar's fender.

Production for 1955

Sales for 1955 were better than for the previous year. Unfortunately, the improvement was small. A total of 5,142 were sold: 953 FL, 853 FLE, 63 FLH, 2,013 FLF, 220 FLEF, and 1,040 FLHF. No one really knows for sure why the sales increased, but my guess is that it's due largely to the introduction

Above left: Late in the year, Harley released a hotter engine, in the form of the FLH Super Sport. The FLH's polished and flowed intake tract gave it 10 percent more horsepower.

Above: Late 1954 and 1955 bikes were fitted with new-style thick aluminum D-rings with only six mounting-screw holes in each, so only six hex-head screws were used to secure each rocker cover to its cylinder head. The six-screw arrangement did not seal well, so new 12-hole D-rings were used on 1956 and later Panheads.

Left: For 1955 the lock on the toolbox was replaced by a wing nut.

Rather than two, this bike has three removable covers. The frontmost and smallest only appear on bikes fitted with the new, optional compensating sprocket (an engine shock absorber). The center cover is the primary inspection cover, and the rearmost is the clutch cover. Both rear covers are painted black unless the optional chrome-plated covers are ordered.

Right: Like the late-1954 Hydra-Glides, the 1955 Hydra-Glides were fitted with a straight-leg frame similar to the one on the last Knuckleheads, rather than the wishbone-style frame used on all the previous Panheads. At the same time, Harley reverted to fitting the Knuckle-style front crash bars.

of the new factory hot-rod, the Super Sport FLH. Even though it was introduced in the middle of the production run and was a bit more expensive, the FLH accounted for 1,103 sales, more than 20 percent of the total.

The 1956 Hydra-Glides

The year 1956 was one of refinement rather than major change. The most distinguishing feature of the 1956 line was a gorgeous new two-tone paint scheme featuring a broad contrasting stripe slashing across the gas tanks.

Models, Prices, and Option Groups
For 1956, the Hydra-Glide was again offered with the FL, FLE, or FLH engine. Each motor was available with hand shift (designated Model FL, FLE, or FLH) or foot shift (designated Model FLF, FLEF, or FLHF). Per usual Harley-Davidson practice, only FL, FLE, or FLH, not the "F" for "foot shift," was stamped into the case as part of the serial number. Police or sidecar gearing was also available as a no-cost option.

Base-model FLs and FLEs retailed for $1,055, and base-model FLHs retailed for $1,123, each just $40 more than the previous year's prices.

This 1956 Hydra-Glide is an FLF model—the last F meaning that it was fitted with a foot shift. Foot-shift twins were fitted with new left tanks that no longer had the lug for the shifter pivot or the mounting holes for the shifter gate, a clutch hand lever on the left handlebar, a spring-assisted clutch booster mounted vertically along the left front down tube, and a foot-shift lever. The clutch-booster cover shown is chrome plated. Chrome booster covers were first offered on new Panheads in 1959, as part of the Chrome Finish Group.

Starting with 1956, the items that had been part of the extra-cost Standard Solo Group (and Utility Solo Group before that) were included in the base price. These items included a black front safety guard, an air cleaner, a jiffy stand, and black wheels with 5.00x16-inch tires. Three new civilian solo option groups were offered to dress up the basic bike.

The Chrome Finish Group was a package of all the most popular dress-up accessories. It retailed for $54 and included the following items:

- chrome front safety guard, rims, headlight, clutch-inspection cover, muffler, exhaust-pipe covers, and instrument-panel cover
- chrome rubber-mounted handlebars
- stainless fork trim (five pieces)
- timer cover
- primary-chain inspection cover
- polished fork sliders, brake side cover, and horn body and cover
- colored plastic grips

The Road Cruiser Group was a package of the basic touring accessories. It retailed for $108 and included:

- deluxe buddy seat #52503-36 (exchange)
- King saddlebags #90994-53
- compensating sprocket (exchange)
- oil-filter assembly
- rear bumper, rear-bumper grille
- solo windshield (choice of all-clear, clear and red, or clear and blue)

For an additional $11, the package came with the super deluxe buddy seat.

The King of the Highway Group included all the basic touring accessories plus much more. It retailed for $191.50 and included

- super deluxe buddy seat 52503-54 (exchange)
- rear bumper, rear-bumper grille
- oil-filter assembly
- compensating sprocket (exchange)
- chrome crossover and dual mufflers
- front hub cap
- directional signals
- front bumper 91075-55
- cigarette lighter
- buddy-seat rail
- chrome luggage carrier and boot guard
- plastic saddlebags (choice of pepper red, atomic blue, or black)
- solo windshield (choice of all-clear, clear and red, or clear and blue).

In this author's opinion, the dramatic tank striping on the 1956 models made it one of the most attractive of the Hydra-Glides. This prime example was restored by Elmer Ehnes.

Shown on a different 1956 FL is the basic style of speedometer introduced in 1956. Changes for that year included the light gold center; the numerals, hash marks, and the company name are all painted in "green Day-Glo" paint on the underside of the glass. This is actually the 1957 version of the speedometer; for 1956 the trip meter tenth-mile numerals should be black on a white background.

The Standard Police Group sold for $65 and included:

- rear-wheel siren
- speedometer hand control
- deluxe solo saddle (exchange), and
- choice of speedster or buckhorn handlebars

Factory Paint Options

For 1956, the Hydra-Glides featured one of the most handsome two-tone paint schemes ever used on a Harley. Tanks were given graceful side stripes that arc up and forward from the lower rear edge of the tank, around and past the same V tank emblem that had been used in 1955.

This scheme was offered in seven standard colors and one optional color. Standard were: Pepper Red with white tank stripes and red fenders, Atomic Blue with Champion Yellow tank stripes and blue fenders, Champion Yellow with black tank stripes and yellow fenders, Black with Champion Yellow tank stripes and black fenders, Silver (Police Group only), and White (Police Group only). Available for $5 extra was a scheme of Flamboyant Metallic Green with white tank stripes and green fenders. Though not listed on the order blanks, gas tanks could be ordered in standard

colors without tank stripes, at no extra cost, according to *The Enthusiast* of September 1955.

Chassis Updates and Detail Changes

There were a few updates and changes to note for 1956, but all were minor.

Speedometer Probably the most noticeable was the facelift given the speedometer. Overall, it was similar to the 1955 speedometer except that the lower face was now painted a "light gold" and the numerals, 2-mile-per-hour division marks, and the words "Harley-Davidson" were painted in "green Day-Glo" on the underside of the glass.

Frame The frame was also slightly modified. The coil-mounting-block holes were ⅜ inch (rather than ⁵⁄₁₆ inch), and a stainless-steel cover was added to the steering-head lock. This frame was used in 1956 and 1957.

Decal Starting in 1956, the Harley-Davidson patent decal was no longer placed on the left side of the oil tank. For 1956 and later, it was on the front of the oil tank, hidden from view by the seat-post tube. On FLH models, a new FLH decal was used on both sides of the oil tank. The FLH decal consisted of a large red V on a white shield with the black letters "FLH" over both. This decal was used on all 1956–1960 FLHs.

Windshield For 1956 the optional solo windshield was slightly revised and was also offered for the first time with red or blue lower panels. Of course, the clear panels were also available.

Motor Updates

Unlike the chassis, the 1956 Panhead motor was given quite a few changes. Oddly, most of the changes were actually further refinements of major changes made the previous year.

Sprocket-Shaft and Bearings The Timken sprocket-shaft bearings and new sprocket shaft that were introduced in 1955 were indeed stronger than the older parts, but the design made the inner bearing difficult to remove for servicing. The inner bearing seated against a shoulder on the left flywheel, so the shaft had to be removed from the flywheel before the bearing could be pressed off the shaft. To correct the problem, Harley-Davidson engineers released a new set of left lower-end components. The new left flywheel lacked the bearing shoulder that had been used on the 1955 flywheel. Instead, the bearing shoulder was added to the new sprocket shaft, spacing the bearing away from the flywheel just enough to allow a bearing puller to get a grip on the bearing. The sprocket-shaft's key slot was also made

deeper. This sprocket shaft was used through 1964. The new left flywheel was used through 1960.

D-Rings New versions of the ¾-inch, cast-aluminum D-rings were fitted for 1956. These new D-rings had 12 mounting holes for a better valve-cover oil seal. Each cover was fastened by 12 hex-head cap screws. These D-rings and screws are correct for 1956–1965 Panheads.

Check-Valve Spring Problems with oil draining from the oil tank through the lifters into the crankcase were finally solved by fitting a new check-valve spring in the oil pump. This new oil pump was used through mid-1962.

"Victory" Cam for the FLH For 1956 FLH motors were fitted with the hot new "Victory" camshaft. The new cam had higher lift (1.342 inches versus 1.334 inches) and narrower lobes (1.075 inches versus 1.10 inches). In combination with the polished and flowed ports and higher-compression pistons that were also included in the FLH package, the new cam gave the FLH 12 percent more power than the FL. This cam was used in 1956–1969 FLH motors.

Air Cleaner A new-style air cleaner was also fitted to the 1956 Hydra-Glides. The new stainless-steel cover was still 7 inches in diameter but was fastened by a chromed center screw, rather than by J-slots on the cover's edge. Also, the data plate that had been riveted to earlier air-cleaner covers was no longer fitted. Instead, the information from the data plate was stamped into the cover. Inside the cover was a new, replaceable filter element made of corrugated paper (rather than oiled copper) backed with wire mesh. This new style of air cleaner was used through 1965.

Other Motor Adjustments Many top-end parts that had been introduced in 1955 were also replaced in 1956. The 1956 cylinder heads were entirely new castings with nine fins on the pushrod side (instead of six), 12 valve-cover mounting holes, and the casting mark "16700 56 FRONT" or "16701 56 REAR" cast into the head between the pushrod holes. Now, however, the casting mark was on the top of the head in the area covered by the valve cover. FLH heads had polished and flowed intake ports. These new heads were also used for 1957.

This FLF shows the foot-shift mechanism introduced in late 1951 as an option. The round chrome or stainless cover on the left side hides the horn's power pack.

The engine's bottom end was revised for 1956 to make it easier to service. Among the new parts were the left flywheel and sprocket shaft. The engine also was given new cylinder-head castings, 12-hole D-rings, and a new Victory camshaft for FLH models.

A new-style air-filter cover was fitted for 1956. A center screw fastened the cover to the filter plate, rather than the "J-slots" used on previous filters.

Production for 1956

Sales increased again for 1956, to 5,806. Included in this total are 856 FL, 671 FLE, 224 FLH, 1,578 FLF, 162 FLEF, and 2,315 FLHF. In its first full year of production, the FLH had risen to be the new star of the lineup, accounting for almost half of total sales.

The 1957 Hydra-Glides

For 1957 the Hydra-Glide rode in the shadow of its new little brother, the first Sportster. Harley engineers had been busy getting the Sportster ready for production and were hard at work on the next big round of changes to the Panhead, scheduled for 1958, so few changes were made to the Big Twin for 1957. And those that were made were largely cosmetic.

Models, Prices, and Option Groups

For 1957, the FLE Traffic-Combination motor was dropped, leaving only the FL and FLH Hydra-Glides in the lineup. Each motor was available with hand shift (designated Model FL or FLH) or

The Deluxe Solo Saddle shown on the bike is the correct type for 1955 and later Panheads.

The new tank emblems were made of plastic.

foot shift (designated Model FLF or FLHF). Per usual Harley-Davidson practice, only FL or FLH, not the "F" for "foot shift," was stamped into the case as part of the serial number. Police or sidecar gearing was also available as a no-cost option.

Base-model FLs retailed for $1,167, and base-model FLHs for $1,243, each 10 percent higher than the previous year's prices. As was the case for

Hydra-Glide looks were updated once again for 1957 with new tank striping and emblems. This example was restored by John Viljoen and Scott Lange.

Shown here is the 1957 speedometer. It was like the 1956 version, except that the tenth-mile numerals were red on a black background for 1957.

1956, base models were equipped with a black front safety guard, an air cleaner, a jiffy stand, and black wheels with 5.00x16-inch tires, but three civilian solo option groups were offered to dress up the basic bike.

The Chrome Finish Group was a package of all the most popular dress-up accessories. It retailed for $64.90 and included the following items:
- chrome front safety guard, rims, headlight, clutch-inspection cover, timer cover, primary-chain-inspection cover, muffler, exhaust-pipe covers, and instrument-panel cover
- chrome rubber-mounted handlebars
- stainless fork trim (five pieces)
- polished fork sliders, brake side cover, and horn body and cover
- colored plastic grips
- oil filter (attached)

The Road Cruiser Group was a package of the basic touring accessories. It retailed for $117.35 and included:
- deluxe buddy seat (in place of standard saddle)

- leather white-welt king saddlebags 90994-53A (attached)
- Hydra-Glide windshield (choice of blue, red, or clear)
- compensating sprocket (in place of rigid)
- 91007-52 rear bumper
- 91023-52 rear bumper grille, and
- 49153-36 chrome rear safety guard

If the buyer wanted to upgrade to the super deluxe buddy seat, the package retailed for $128.35. If the buyer wanted the deluxe solo saddle, the package was $103.85. If the buyer preferred plastic saddlebags in place of the leather ones, the package cost $119.35.

The King of the Highway Group included all the basic touring accessories plus much more. It retailed for $192 and included:

- super deluxe buddy seat 52503-54 (exchange)
- 90651-54 plastic saddlebags and carrier
- Hydra-Glide windshield (choice of blue, red, or clear)
- 91007-52 rear bumper
- 91023-52 rear bumper grille
- compensating sprocket (in place of rigid)
- dual muffler with crossover
- 43303-49 front hub cap
- 68550-50 directional signals
- 91575-49A buddy seat rail
- 53403-52 chrome luggage carrier
- 65700-38 chrome boot guard
- 49153-36 chrome rear safety guard

Even this comprehensive package could be tuned to owner tastes. If the buyer wanted a deluxe solo seat in place of the super deluxe buddy seat, the package price was $169. If he preferred the deluxe buddy seat, it was $182.50.

The Standard Police Group sold for $65 and included:

- rear-wheel siren
- speedometer hand control
- deluxe solo saddle (exchange)
- choice of speedster or buckhorn handlebars

Factory Paint Options

An all-new two-tone paint style was standard for 1957. Fenders and the sides of the tank were painted one color, while a panel atop the tank was painted in a contrasting color.

Four standard color combinations were offered: Pepper Red with Black tank panels and red fenders, Skyline Blue with Birch White tank panels and blue fenders, Birch White with Black tank panels and white fenders, and Black with Pepper Red tank panels and Black fenders.

Optional at no extra charge were the following solid colors and combinations: Police Silver (Police Group only), Birch White (solid or with black tank panels), any standard color without tank panels, fenders painted to match the tank

Tank tops and sides were painted in contrasting colors for 1957. Shown is the combination of black with pepper red tank panels. This 1957 Hydra-Glide was restored by Elmer Ehnes.

This style of Deluxe Buddy Seat was correct for 1954–1956 Hydra-Glides. The correct seat for 1957–1960 was very similar to this except that it had a tooled leather skirt with two nickel dots on each side.

For 1957, the rocker covers were made of polished aluminum, rather than stainless steel.

Above: Inside the engine, new pushrods and exhaust-valve guides were fitted for 1957.

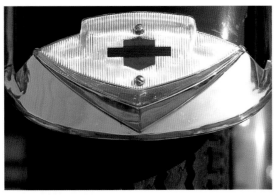

Above right and right: A plastic fender tip was also standard for 1957. This fender tip and the side-trim strips that extend back from it were used for 1957 and 1958.

panel. And optional for a $5 extra charge was Metallic Midnight Blue with Birch White tank panels and blue fenders.

Chassis Updates and Detail Changes

For its last year in production, all the changes to the Hydra-Glide chassis were cosmetic.

Tank Emblems Those new-style tank panels on the 1957 Hydra-Glides framed all-new tank emblems. For the first time on the Panhead line, the tank emblems were plastic instead of metal.

Each was a rounded disc with a silver-colored rim and a background divided in quadrants (two gold, two red). The name "Harley-Davidson" was printed over the top of the disc in red block letters in two lines. This emblem was used for 1957 only. (The 1958 emblem is similar, but the colors were black and gold.)

Front Fender Tip Complementing the tank emblems was a new tip for the front fender. It, too, was plastic. The fender tip was decorated with the bar-and-shield logo in red and a silver or gold V (both colors are seen on NOS parts). New stainless-steel trim strips extended back from the fender tip

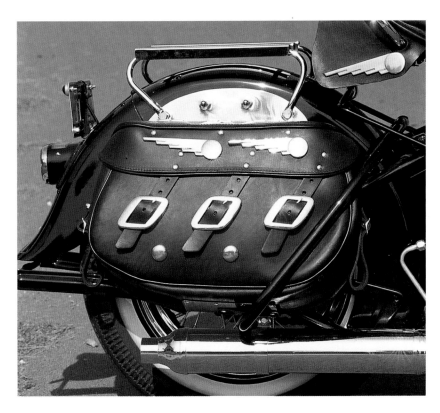

to the fork sliders. This fender tip is correct only for 1957 and 1958. The side trim strips continued to be used with the new fender tip introduced in 1959 and used through 1965.

Speedometer Small changes were made to the speedometer as well. The 1957 style Stewart-Warner speedometer was the same "green Day-Glo" design as the 1956, except that the tenth-mile numerals were painted red on a black background. In addition, a new, thinner speedometer cable was fitted from the transmission to the speedometer.

Motor Updates

As for the chassis, changes to the 1957 Panhead engine were few and superficial. The most noticeable of these was that the stainless-steel rocker covers that had been used since 1949 were replaced for 1957 with stamped aluminum covers that are otherwise the same as earlier covers. Aluminum covers are correct for 1957–1965 Panheads.

Several small internal changes refined the engine. New pushrods were fitted that were shorter overall so they could be adjusted down and removed easier. Starting February 1, 1957, new steel-alloy exhaust-valve guides were introduced to replace the bronze guides used since 1950. The new exhaust-valve guides were "threaded" inside to trap oil and improve lubrication. The intake guides were not threaded because threaded guides would have allowed too much oil to leak into the combustion chamber. Starting with motor number 57FLH4444, new, stronger valve springs are fitted to all FLH motors.

Options and Accessories

For 1957 the optional leather King Size, Fringed King, and Streamliner saddlebags were modified to make them lockable but quickly detachable. Their new bag hangers had two studs and a U-shaped padlock fitting to secure the bag to the hanger. These bags are also equipped with "never sag" expanders.

New on the options list were the extra-large Big Bertha saddlebags, available for 1957 only. Like the other 1957 leather bags, these bags had the quick-disconnect leather bag mounts and "never sag" expanders.

Harley's inventory must finally have run out of nickel comets, so the optional black Royalite hard plastic saddlebags got a facelift in 1957. The new bags were trimmed with a red "shark" or "jet" overlaid on a slanted silver oval.

Further evidence that the comets were finally out of stock: The Deluxe Buddy seat was restyled with a tooled-leather skirt with large nickel dots on each side replacing the comets.

Above left: The 1957 Speed King bags are like those used from 1954–1956, except the newer model could be quickly detached from its hanger.

Above: Chrome-plated dashes were first offered on new Hydra-Glides for 1957.

On foot-shift machines, the clutch lever was on the left bar, and the brake lever was moved to the right bar. The push button activates the horn.

The bags may visually conceal the rigid rear, but one ride on a rugged road would quickly expose the truth: a spring seat was no longer enough in 1957.

With a highly refined motor and a good front suspension, the Panhead really needed a good rear suspension. It would get it for the next year.

Production for 1957

Sales dropped to 5,616 for 1957. This total includes 1,579 FL, 164 FLH, 1,259 FLF, and 2,614 FLHF. Once again, almost half the total was the hot-rod FLH. More interesting, more than half of the FLs sold were hand-shift bikes, whereas hand-shift bikes were just a minuscule portion of the FLHs sold. Once again, though, the "F" for "foot shift" wasn't stamped on the motor. Because there is no way to conclusively document that a given bike was delivered from the factory as a hand-shift bike (unless the owner possesses the original Harley delivery documents), don't get suckered into thinking that such a bike should be worth more than any other 1957 FLH. It is so easy to convert a bike from foot shift to hand shift that there could easily be more hand-shift 1958 FLHs today than Harley-Davidson originally built.

During eight years of production, the Hydra-Glides gained weight, power, better lifters, and a stronger bottom end. What it really needed was rear suspension. And that's the headline feature of the Hydra-Glide's successor, the Duo-Glide of 1958.

Chapter 3

The 1958–1964 Duo-Glides

Rear suspension was the big news for 1958. Harley engineers redesigned the whole rear end to use a pair of shock absorbers and a swing arm to really improve the ride. Shown on this well-dressed Duo-Glide are the correct black saddlebags with the correct trim: the red "shark" on a polished oval. Tool boxes on Duo-Glides were moved forward and stood on end to leave room for the new shock absorbers.

While rigid frames and sprung seats provided all the rear suspension anyone had expected in the 1930s and 1940s, the Panhead's hardtail rear end was clearly old-fashioned by the late 1950s. Even the outsized saddlebags and crash bars that riders fitted onto their Hydra-Glides could no longer hide that fact. Worse yet, the new Sportster of 1957 had rear suspension, as had its predecessors, the Models K and KH. How come the lesser twins had rear suspension while the King of the Highway was still a hardtail? Big Twin riders rightfully felt left out. That is, until the fall of 1957, with the introduction of Panhead Part III, the Duo-Glide, for 1958.

This unrestored 1958 Duo-Glide was fitted with most of the items in the King of the Highway option group, including the Super Deluxe Buddy Seat with the correct twin-tube handrail that was new for 1958, dual exhaust, plastic saddlebags, and many other items. Several items on this super-nice machine are not correct: the bags should be black, the trim strip on the lower back edge of this bike's front fender is correct for 1949–1957, and the cylinders should be painted silver. For 1958, new heads were fitted that have noticeably longer fins. Attached to these heads is a new version of the O-ring manifold that is cast of aluminum.

The 1958 Duo-Glides

The "Duo" in Duo-Glide was Harley's acknowledgment of the most important update to its Big Twin since the Hydra-Glide front end of 1949: a swing-arm rear suspension with a hydraulically damped shock absorber on each side. For the first time the rear suspension was as good as the front.

What difference did those rear shocks make? A lot, actually. A smoother ride on all roads and a real reduction in the pummeling you'd take on the bumpy ones, which turned a really good long-haul bike for its time into a great one. With suspenders fore and aft, the Panhead was transformed into the undisputed King of the American Road.

That suspension also forced a restyle of the whole rear end that made the old Big Twin seem modern again. As a bonus, the Duo-Glide introduced hydraulic rear brakes for better stopping power. Once again, Harley had spent its money to make its flagship machine more civilized.

Models, Prices, and Option Groups

First-year Duo-Glides were available with the FL and FLH engines. Each motor was available with hand shift (designated Model FL or FLH) or foot shift (designated Model FLF or FLHF). Per usual Harley-Davidson practice, only FL or FLH, not the "F" for "foot shift," was stamped into the case as part of the serial number. Police or sidecar gearing was also available as a no-cost option.

Base-model FLH Duo-Glides retailed for $1,320, and base-model FL Duo-Glides for $1,255, both about 10 percent higher than the previous year's prices. Base models were equipped with a black front safety guard, an air cleaner, a jiffy stand, and black wheels with 5.00x16-inch tires, but seven solo and two police option groups were offered to dress up the basic bike.

The Chrome Finish Group F-1 was a package of all the most popular dress-up accessories. It included the following items: chrome front safety guard, rubber-mounted chrome handlebars (choice of speedster or buckhorn), chrome rims, chrome headlight, stainless-steel fork trim (five pieces), chrome clutch inspection cover, chrome timer cover, chrome primary-chain inspection cover, chrome muffler, polished fork sliders, polished brake side cover, polished horn body and cover, chrome exhaust-pipe covers, colored plastic handlebar grips, chrome instrument-panel cover, oil filter (attached), and chrome caps for rear shock absorber (with two clamps with screws, nuts, and washers).

The Road Cruiser Group F-2 was a package of the basic touring accessories. It included the following:
- 52503-58 deluxe buddy seat (in place of standard saddle)
- chrome front bumper, rear safety guard, and front parking lamps (white)
- 90851-58 pair of plastic saddlebags and carrier
- windshield (choice of blue, red, or clear)
- compensating sprocket (in place of rigid)

Road Cruiser Group F-3 was the same as F-2 except that the deluxe solo seat replaced the buddy seat. Road Cruiser Group F-4 was also the same as F-2 except that the super deluxe buddy seat was substituted.

The King of the Highway Group F-5 was the deluxe touring package. It included:
- 52504-58 super deluxe buddy seat
- 66373-54 chrome battery cover
- 90851-58 pair of plastic saddlebags and carrier
- windshield (choice of 57998-56 blue, 57999-56 red, 58002-49 clear)
- 59885-48 chrome rear-fender tip
- 59235-48 rear-fender flap
- 40277-55a compensating sprocket (exchange)
- 65425-58 dual mufflers with crossover
- 43303-49 front hub cap (attached)
- 68550-58 directional signals
- 91575-49a buddy seat rail
- 65700-38 chrome boot guard
- 49150-58 chrome rear safety guard
- 53403-58 chrome luggage carrier (not attached)
- 91075-58 front bumper (not attached)
- 43895-56 chrome axle and fork stud caps (attached)

Group F-6 substituted the deluxe solo seat, and Group F-7 substituted the super deluxe buddy seat.

The Standard Police Group FP-1 included:
- front-wheel siren
- speedometer hand control (attached)
- deluxe solo saddle (exchange)
- rigid-mounted buckhorn handlebars

Group FP-2 also included a foot control for the siren.

Factory Paint Options
A new paint scheme with two-tone tanks and fenders was standard for 1958. The tanks were fitted with round plastic tank badges, similar to those in 1958. The top of the tank was painted in a contrasting color that wraps around the top of the emblems to cover the top half of the front part of the tank.

The following standard color combinations were available: Skyline Blue tank top with Birch White sides and mudguards with white top and blue sides, Calypso Red tank top with Birch White sides and mudguards with white top and red sides, Sabre Gray Metallic tank top with Birch

The speedometer for 1958 was the same as 1957's, except the tenth-mile numerals are black on a white background (rather than red on a black background). The black knob ahead of the speedometer is for the steering damper. All 1958 Duo-Glides were fitted with steering dampers, but it was found that they caused a problem with high-speed wobbles if the damper was tightened, so they were only fitted to sidecar models or on special orders from 1959 on. Plastic tank emblems (left) for 1958 were very similar to the 1957 emblems, except that the colors were black and gold. Note that the valve-cover D-rings should be unpainted aluminum, and the valve-cover screws should be hex-head.

White sides and mudguards with white top and gray sides, and black tank top with Birch White sides and mudguards with white top and black sides. Police Silver with any standard color solid (without tank panels) was available at no extra charge. Police Silver and overall Birch White were available to police only.

Chassis Updates and Detail Changes
Getting that swing arm and shocks rear suspension on the old chassis required more than just a

Whitewall tires were first offered as an option on new machines in 1958. They look great with the two-tone paint scheme for 1958.

Far right: Duo-Glides were fitted with the same oval taillight that had been introduced in 1955. This style of taillight was used through the end of the Panhead line and was always painted the color of the fender.

Right: This style of front-fender tip was used for two years: first on the 1957 Hydra-Glide and then on the 1958 Duo-Glide. The Aristocrat front bumper shown here was new for 1958 and remained on the option list through 1965.

The Duo-Glide was the first Harley-Davidson Big Twin with hydraulic rear brakes. 1958 was the first year for the smooth toolbox cover (previous covers had four raised ribs), but a wing bolt was still used to close the cover. This bike is equipped with the optional Aristocrat rear bumper that was introduced in mid-1958 and was a later-model (1959–1965) rear-fender tip. The correct tip for 1958 is the earlier, more rounded style, but it is possible that some very late 1958 bikes were shipped with the tip shown.

new rear section for the frame and attaching parts. Most of the chassis was new for 1958. In fact, more was changed that year than in any other five years combined.

The Duo-Glide Frame The 1958 Duo-Glide frame was a straight-leg cradle frame with twin down tubes, large-diameter backbone tube, and vertical seat post behind the motor, like the last of the Hydra-Glide frames. From the seat post back, however, everything was new. Bridging all the tubes at the rear was a swing-arm-pivot forging on each side, with a tube connecting the two forgings together. The rear transmission mount was welded to this tube. Rear suspension was courtesy of a conventional, forked swing arm.

The mount for the teardrop toolbox disappeared with the old lower rear tube on the right side, so new mounts were added to the rear vertical tube and lower forging on the right side, to which the toolbox attached vertically, with the larger end down. Also, the "loop" sidecar-mount

forgings were no longer welded to the front down tubes. (On 1958 and later Duo-Glides, the sidecars mount to forgings that are held to the motorcycle frame by U-bolts.)

The left and right top rear tubes now terminated at the front of the shock-mount forgings, and another tube bridged the gap between the right and left forgings at the top. Each shock-mount forging had two mounting lugs, a large one for the top shock mount (located just above the vertical tube from the lower forging) and a smaller one toward the aft end of the forging for the new alloy fender-support arm.

The Duo-Glide frame became known as the "step-down" frame because the upper-shock-mount forging bent down noticeably between the top shock mount and the cross brace just in front of it. Harley-Davidson engineers must have gotten it right the first time in designing this frame; it was used without noteworthy change from 1958 to 1964.

Shock Absorbers The new shock absorber assemblies consisted of a shock absorber and spring sheathed in a chrome cover. These shocks were usually fitted with the optional chromed dome caps over the top of the shock mounts (available with the Chrome Finish Group). This style of shock was used from 1958 to 1964.

New Crash Bars
Both front and rear crash bars were redesigned for the Duo-Glide frame. The one-piece tubular front safety guard mounted with a single bolt (rather than with two U-bolts) to a new bracket between the frame down tubes. This new guard is correct for 1958–1965 Panheads.

Duo-Glide rear safety guards were a two-piece guard replacing the Hydra-Glide's one-piece. This style of guard is correct from 1958 to 1964. These guards were optional and could be ordered in black or chrome-plated finishes.

Oil Tank and Filter
A new oil tank was designed to fit the new frame. This oil tank was similar to the horseshoe oil tanks that had been used on the OHV twins since 1940, but with two battery tie-down tabs welded to the tank at the back of the battery well. (The battery tie-downs on hardtail machines had bolted to the rear fender.) This new oil tank is correct for 1958–1964 Panheads.

This well-equipped Duo-Glide was fitted with the optional spot lamps, front running lights, control-coil covers, and rubber-mounted handlebars.

Optional control-coil covers contrast nicely with the chrome dash and handlebars.

The oil-filter assembly required a new bracket and oil-return line to fit the swing-arm frame. This new filter assembly was used on 1958–1964 Panheads.

Toolboxes Toolboxes on Harley's OHV twins had been teardrop shaped and horizontally mounted since the 1940 Knucklehead. This changed for 1958: the right shock absorber cuts diagonally through the space occupied by the old toolbox, standing the toolbox on its large end, just ahead of the shock absorber. The toolbox was still teardrop, but no longer with ribs stamped into the cover.

Some early 1958 toolboxes were held closed by a wing bolt, but most 1958 toolboxes and all later boxes were closed by a screw. As with previous toolboxes, the 1958 toolboxes were painted black. The Harley-Davidson order blanks did not list chrome covers as optional until 1959, but it is possible that they were available for new bike orders in late 1958.

Chain Guard Replacing the rigid-mounted rear-chain guard that had been used since the Knucklehead of 1940 was a new rear-chain guard designed to move up and down with the wheel. The new guard was painted black and was used through 1962.

Rear Fender and Supports The old rear-fender mounts could no longer be used with the new swing-arm frame because the old fender had braces that mounted to the axle plates. For the Duo-Glide, new fender mounts were designed to mount the fender rigidly to the upper part of the frame while leaving it independent of the swing arm. These new mounts consisted of twin alloy rear-fender supports that attached to the frame's upper-shock-mount forgings and swept back horizontally along the fender, fastening to it with four straight-slot screws on each side. These fender supports were used from 1958 to 1976, but the straight-slot screws were used only for 1958.

The fender was also redesigned to go with the new mounts. The new fender was still a two-piece stamping with the front and rear stampings connected by a hinge, but the skirts of the fender were no longer smooth. They now had a ridge stamped in relief near the top of the skirt that followed the curvature of the fender and a dimple on each side near the front for the fender braces. This rear fender was used through 1964. For 1958 only, the rounded chrome fender tip that had been optional since 1948 was used with the new-style fender.

Fork The stem and top triple tree for both the fixed- and adjustable-rake forks were modified to fit the new frame. These new fork assemblies were used only for 1958 and 1959. The forks are otherwise the same as on previous Panheads.

"Duo-Glide" Fender Badges The 1958 Duo-Glide used 1957's same front fender tip and side trim strips, but a new chromed Duo-Glide emblem was mounted to each side of the fender, and the small stainless-steel trim strip that protected the lower rear rim of the fender was gone. Duo-Glide emblems were standard from 1958 to 1964.

"Juice" Brakes Along with the new rear suspension, the 1958 Panhead was given a hydraulically actuated rear brake. The new system was modeled after the hydraulic rear brakes that had first been fitted to the 1951 Servicar. This system eliminated the need for brake rods and crossovers and worked so well that it was carried over (with only minor changes) through 1971.

The black-painted drum had an 8-inch inside diameter and was made of stamped steel. It was secured to the wheel with five screws and the drive sprocket and dust ring was secured to the drum by ⅛-inch rivets. The shoes for this hub were 1 5⁄16 inches wide and had linings specially formulated to work with the steel hub. The linings were glued to the shoes, and the metal part of these shoes was painted gray.

The brake backing plate was 8½ inches in diameter and had a bell-shaped reinforcement plate riveted with five rivets to a like-shaped recess stamped into the backing plate. This backing plate was used from 1958 to 1963 and was painted black.

There must have been problems with the stamped drums, however, because starting with engine number 58FL3441, a new, cast-iron drum and new, 1⁵⁄₁₆-inch shoes with linings formulated for the iron hub were fitted. (*Shop Dope* No. 398 lists about 70 other individual bikes with lower serial numbers that were fitted with the new drum at the factory.) This new drum was used in 1958 and 1959. The metal part of the shoes were painted black to distinguish them from the steel hub's gray-painted shoes. These shoes were used through 1962.

Speedometer

Speedometer The speedometer head was changed slightly for 1958. It was a "green Day-Glo" design similar to 1957's, except the tenth-mile numerals were painted black on a white background (instead of red on a black background).

Motor Updates

For a year in which The Motor Company introduced a new chassis, there were a surprising number of changes to the engine and drive train.

Heads and Intake Manifold Cylinder heads with wider and thicker fins were introduced for 1958. As before, the FLH heads were the same as the FL heads, except the intake ports were flowed and polished and heavier valve springs were fitted on the FLH. In mid-1958, however, the FLH machines began to be fitted with stellite-faced valves. (FL models were not given stellite valves until 1960.) These heads were used from 1958 to 1962.

The 1958 O-ring intake manifold's only change was from cast iron to cast aluminum. This manifold was unpainted and was fitted from 1958 to 1965.

Bottom-End Updates

Minor changes were also made to the crankcases. The left crankcase's rear motor mount was redesigned to allow mounting of the new voltage regulator (regulators were first fitted to non-police machines in 1958).

The right case was redesigned to accommodate a larger-diameter pinion-bearing race and a new roller bearing for the cam gear (replacing a bronze bushing). Also, the generator mounting holes were enlarged (from ¼ inch to ⁵⁄₁₆ inches). Both cases were used from 1958 to 1962. A new gear cover with ⁵⁄₁₆-inch generator-mounting holes was introduced to go with the revised right crankcase. The new gear case was used from 1958 to 1962.

The inner primary-chain housing was modified to position the breather-pipe hole where the breather pipe emerged from the crankcase. The new inner cover was painted black and was used from 1958 to 1963. (Covers for foot-shift bikes differed slightly from covers for hand-shift bikes.)

New clutch hub bearings and their retainer were also introduced, consisting of 20 rollers instead of the previous 30 ball bearings. The new bearings were used from 1958 to the end of the Panheads.

Exhaust Two pipes in the standard single-exhaust system had to be updated for use with the Duo-Glide frame: the rear header and the Y-pipe. The new Y-pipe was 16½ inches long (the old-style pipe was 10½ inches long) to accommodate the swing-arm frame. The rear header pipe was slightly changed to fit the new Y-pipe. The Y-pipe was chrome plated, and the rear header was silver painted.

Two pipes and the mufflers were also revised for the optional dual-exhaust system. The right and left rear pipes were both longer, but the mufflers were shorter versions of the single-exhaust muffler. Pipes and mufflers were chrome plated. The dual exhaust was included in the King of the Highway Group, or it could be ordered separately.

Model 58 Generator A new 6-volt generator made its debut on the Duo-Glide. Earlier standard generators had been three-brush designs that operated without a separate voltage regulator. The new Model 58 generator was a two-brush design requiring an external voltage regulator to limit current output. The regulator mounted on the right side of the motor, aft of the rear tappet block. The generator was mounted by ⅜ inch hex-head screws (instead of Phillips-head screws). The new generator put out more current at a lower rpm than did previous generators and was used through 1960.

Radio-equipped motorcycles were equipped with the same Model 51 two-brush generator with attached cooling fan and separate voltage regulator that had been fitted to all radio-equipped Panheads since 1952, but the generator drive gears for both the standard and radio generators were changed for 1958, from 1.022 inches to 1 inch in diameter. This generator and drive gear were used through 1964.

Options and Accessories

Whitewall tires were first offered from the factory for the 1958 season, so they are really correct only on 1958 and later Panheads.

The optional chrome rail for the optional Deluxe and Super Deluxe buddy seats was redesigned in mid-1958 to a new "twin-tube" design. The old-style rail (consisting of a single

For its second year, the Duo-Glide was restyled. This beautiful 1959 FLH was restored by John Viljoen and Scott Lange.

tube that wraps around behind the seat) was offered in early 1958, so either style is correct for 1958, but only the new-style rail is correct for 1959 and later. Also, the Buddy Seat helper springs were revised to fit the new frame.

The optional, bullet-shaped turn signals were given redesigned mounts for 1958. These new turn signals were used through 1962.

The Duo-Glide continued to offer the Royalite plastic saddlebags. The bags themselves were the same as the late Hydra-Glide bags, with revised mounts for the Duo-Glide frame. Only black bags are correct for 1958, but black and white bags are correct for 1959 and later. (White bags were later offered to retrofit to 1958 and earlier models, but they were not available on the new machines.)

A new, optional "Aristocrat" front bumper was introduced in 1958 that matched the style of the "twin-tube" Buddy Seat handrail. The Aristocrat front bumper was offered from 1958 through the end of the Panhead line. A matching Aristocrat rear bumper was introduced later in the 1958 production year. It is also correct for 1958 and later Panheads.

Production for 1958
Despite a minor recession during the year, 1958 Panhead sales were up by about 7.5 percent from the previous year. Harley-Davidson built 1,591 FL, 1,299 FLF, 195 FLH, and 2,953 FLHF. As before, about half the FL models were still hand shift, compared to relatively few of the FLH models.

The 1959 Duo-Glides

Model year 1959 brought little in the way of changes to the Duo-Glide, though it did introduce a new look, courtesy of a handsome, new two-tone paint scheme and new tank emblems.

Models, Prices, and Option Groups
Second-year Duo-Glides were available with the FL and FLH engines. Each motor was available with hand shift (designated Model FL or FLH) or foot shift (designated Model FLF or FLHF). Per usual H-D practice, only FL or FLH, not the "F" for "foot shift," was stamped into the case as part of the serial number. Police or sidecar gearing was also available as a no-cost option.

Base-model 1959 FLH Duo-Glides retailed for $1,345, and base-model FL Duo-Glides for $1,280, both $25 higher than the previous year. Base models were equipped with a black front safety guard, an air cleaner, a jiffy stand, and black wheels with 5.00x16-inch tires, but the company offered no fewer than 13 solo and two police option groups.

The Chrome Finish Group F-1 was a package of all the most popular dress-up accessories. It included the following items:

- 49038-58 chrome front safety guard
- rubber-mounted chrome handlebars (choice of speedster or buckhorn)
- two chrome rims, chrome headlight, clutch-inspection cover, timer cover, primary-chain-inspection cover, muffler, exhaust-pipe covers, instrument-panel cover, clutch-booster-spring cover, and tool-box cover
- stainless-steel fork trim (five pieces)
- polished fork sliders and brake side cover
- polished chrome horn cover and trumpet
- colored plastic handlebar grip
- soil filter (attached)
- chrome caps for rear shock absorber and clamps with screws nuts and washers

The Road Cruiser Group F-2 was a package of the basic touring accessories. It included:

- deluxe buddy seat (in place of standard saddle)
- chrome front bumper and rear safety guard
- pair of white plastic saddlebags and carrier
- windshield (choice of 57998-56 blue, 57999-56 red, or 58002-49 clear)
- compensating sprocket (in place of rigid)
- rear bumper
- rear chain oiler

Road Cruiser Group F-2A was the same as #F-2 but with pair of black plastic saddlebags instead of white.

Road Cruiser Group F-3 was same as #F-2 but with a deluxe solo saddle in place of the deluxe buddy seat. Road Cruiser Group F-3A was the same as #F-3 but with pair of black saddlebags instead of white.

Road Cruiser Group F-4 was also the same as F-2 but substituted the super deluxe buddy seat. Road Cruiser Group F-4A was the same as #F-4 but with 90851-58A black plastic saddlebags instead of white.

The King of the Highway Group F-5 was the deluxe touring package. It included:

- super deluxe buddy seat and new-style buddy seat rail
- pair of white plastic saddlebags and carrier
- windshield (choice of 57998-56 blue, 57999-56 red, or 58002-49 clear)
- compensating sprocket (exchange)
- dual mufflers with crossover
- directional signals

Chrome-plated clutch-booster covers were first offered on new machines for 1959.

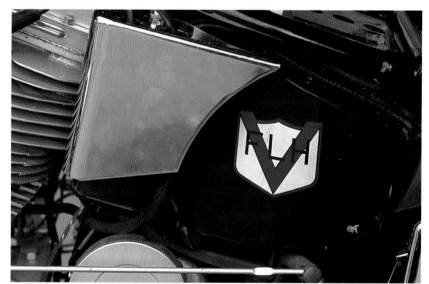

This style of FLH decal was fitted to FLHs from 1956 to 1960.

- chrome battery cover, boot guard, rear safety guard, luggage carrier (not attached), and axle and fork stud caps (attached)
- front bumper (not attached) and rear bumper (not attached)
- rear chain oiler

Group F-5A was the same as F-5 except that it included black plastic saddlebags instead of white.

King of the Highway Group F-6 was the deluxe touring package for solo riders, substituting the deluxe solo saddle for the super deluxe buddy seat. Group F-6A was the same as F-6 with black plastic saddlebags instead of white.

The speedometer for 1959.

Above: Note how much longer the fins of the cylinder head are than those of the cylinders. This style of cylinder head was introduced in 1958.

King of the Highway Group F-7 was the same as F-5 with the deluxe buddy seat substituting for the super deluxe buddy seat. Group F-7A was the same as F-7 except black plastic saddlebags were substituted for white.

The Standard Police Group FP-1 included:
• front-wheel siren
• speedometer hand control (attached)
• deluxe solo saddle (exchange)
• oil filter

Group FP-2 also included a foot control for the siren.

Factory Paint Options

A handsome new two-tone paint scheme graced the 1959 models. Two-tone tanks featured Birch White side panels that wrapped gracefully around the "arrow" tank badge, also new for 1959. The tank emblem was used again for 1960, but a different two-tone scheme was applied.

Starting with 1959 models, Harley-Davidson painted its footboards black. Before this, they had only been Parkerized.

Three standard color combinations were offered: Skyline Blue with Birch White tank side panels, Calypso Red with Birch White tank side panels, and Black with Birch White tank side panels. Optional were Hi-Fi Turquoise with Birch White tank side panels, Hi-Fi Red with Birch White tank side panels, Police Silver (Police Group only), Birch White (Police Group only), and any standard color solid (without tank panels). Fenders on all models were painted in the tank color, without panels.

Chassis Updates and Detail Changes

No significant chassis upgrades were made to the 1959 Duo-Glides. Many small detail changes were made, however.

"Arrow" Tank Emblems The most noticeable of the 1959 detail changes was the new "arrow" tank emblems, consisting of a red disk background pierced by a large chrome arrow. The company name was cast into the shaft of the arrow, with the letters painted red. These emblems were cast of metal instead of the plastic that had been used in 1957–1958. They were fitted to 1969 and 1960 Duo-Glides.

Metal Fender Tips Harley-Davidson also reverted to metal for the new front-fender tips for 1959, replacing the plastic front-fender tips used from 1957 to 1958 with a new, chrome-plated fender tip.

Viewed from straight on, the new tip looked like a large V with a mountain peak rising above it. This style of front-fender tip is correct for 1959 to 1965 Panheads. A matching chromed rear-fender tip was also released in 1959 and was optional for all 1959–1965 Panheads.

Neutral-Indicator Light Foot-shift Duo-Glides were fitted with a revised instrument cover. The only real change was the addition of a new neutral-indicator light covered by a green domed lens. It was positioned to the left and slightly forward of the center mounting bolt on the dash.

This dash style is correct for all foot-shift Panheads from 1959–1961. The instrument panel was painted the same color as the tank unless the Chrome Finish Group was ordered, in which case the panel was chrome plated.

Footboards Starting in 1959, the footboards were painted black. Earlier footboards had been Parkerized but unpainted. For all 1959–1964 Panheads, the footboards were Parkerized (Bonderized) and then painted gloss black.

Clutch Booster-Spring Covers Standard clutch booster-spring covers were cadmium plated for 1959, but a chrome-plated cover was a new option

This new-for-1959 fender tip replaced the plastic tip used for 1957 and 1958.

This new style of chrome-plated rear-fender tip was optional on 1959 and later Panheads.

New, arrow tank emblems and tank panels were the most prominent elements of the 1959 restyle.

Chrome-plated toolbox covers were first listed as an option on new Duo-Glides for 1959, though this bike was not so fitted.

The arrow tank emblem was fitted to 1959 and 1960 Duo-Glides.

Top right: When a customer order included the Chrome Finish Group, the bike's fork sliders and brake backing plate were polished at the factory.

as part of the Chrome Finish Group. Chrome covers could also be ordered individually on the new bike-order form. Chrome-plated covers were optional for 1959–1965, but it is possible that some late-1958 bikes were fitted with chrome covers because the cover's part number has a 1958 prefix.

Toolbox and Straight-Slot Screws The 1959 toolbox was the same vertically mounted, teardrop-shaped, smooth-covered toolbox introduced in 1958, but chrome-plated covers were optional on new machines for the first time in 1959, as part of the Chrome Finish Group or separately from the accessories list (they may have been available earlier from the accessory catalogs or aftermarket sources). Standard covers were painted black.

Finally, the straight-slot screws that fastened the fender to the support for 1958 were replaced from 1959 on with Phillips-slot screws.

Options and Accessories

For 1959, the Royalite plastic saddlebags decorated with the rocket emblems were first offered in white (they had been offered in black since 1957). Both black and white versions of these bags were offered on new 1959–1962 Panheads and are correct for these years. These bags were also offered in the accessory catalogs for later Panheads, but the bags had a winged rocket design, rather than the "jet" or "shark."

To simplify maintenance and tire changes, a new center stand was introduced as an option in 1959, replacing the center stand that had been deleted when the Duo-Glide frame was introduced.

This 1959 Duo-Glide carries the style of deluxe solo seat that is correct for 1955 and later Panheads.

Right: The small chrome cover at the front of the outer primary cover indicates that this FLH was fitted with the optional compensating sprocket.

Far left: Its arrow tank badges and complementary tank panels made the last Panhead of the 1950s one of the most distinctive.

Left: Note the addition of the green indicator light behind the speedometer, on the left side. It was a neutral indicator and was fitted only to foot-shift bikes.

Production for 1959

Production for 1959 was down by about 4 percent from the previous year. Harley-Davidson built 1,201 FLs, 1,222 FLFs, 121 FLHs, and 3,223 FLHFs. For the first time, the high-performance FLH models resoundingly outsold the more sedate FL models. As before, about half the FL models were still hand shift, while relatively few of the FLH models were hand shift.

The stiff competition from Triumph and the rest of the imports heated up even more in 1959. Triumph released its ultimate Harley slayer in the twin-carb T120 Bonneville model. More ominously, Honda motorcycles went on sale in the United States.

For the start of the 1960s, the Duo-Glide was given a substantial facelift when the fork covers were redesigned and replaced by a new, two-piece headlamp nacelle and the paint scheme was updated for the new decade.

The 1960 Duo-Glides

Harley-Davidson designers gave the Duo-Glide a modern new look for the new decade by restyling the front end and paint scheme for 1960. That look, anchored by the heavier styling of the 1960 Duo-Glide's new forks, proved popular and time-less, surviving through the last of the real FLHs in 1984 and being revived on the popular Road King models in the 1990s.

Models, Prices, and Option Groups

The 1960 Duo-Glides were available with the FL and FLH engines. Each motor was available with hand shift (designated Model FL or FLH) or foot shift (designated Model FLF or FLHF). Per usual company practice, only FL or FLH, not the "F" for "foot shift," was stamped into the case as part of the serial number. Police or sidecar gearing was also available as a no-cost option.

Base-model 1960 FLH Duo-Glides retailed for $1,375, and base-model FL Duo-Glides for $1,310, both $30 higher than the previous year. Base models were equipped with a black front safety guard, an air cleaner, a jiffy stand, and black wheels with 5.00x16-inch tires, but no fewer than 13 solo and 3 police option groups were offered to dress up the basic bike.

Chrome Finish Group F-1 was a package of all the most popular dress-up accessories. It included the following items:

- 49038-58 chrome front safety guard
- chrome rubber-mounted handle bars (choice of speedster or buckhorn)
- 43007-40 chrome rims
- 45964-49 stainless-steel fork covers (two pieces)
- 60557-36 chrome clutch inspection cover
- 32589-36 chrome timer cover
- 60573-36 chrome primary-chain-inspection cover
- 65203-58 chrome muffler
- polished fork sliders
- 44141-50 polished brake side cover
- 69022-54 chrome horn cover and 69140-54 chrome horn trumpet
- 65550-58 chrome exhaust-pipe covers
- colored plastic handlebar grips
- 71271-56 chrome instrument-panel cover
- 63800-58 oil filter
- chrome caps for rear shock absorbers
- 38495-58 chrome clutch booster-spring cover
- polished headlamp nacelle and polished handlebar cover

The Road Cruiser Group F-2 was a package of the basic touring accessories. It included:

- 91007-58 rear bumper, 91075-58A front bumper
- 90849-59 white plastic saddle bags and carrier
- windshield (choice of 57996-60 clear, 57998-60 blue, or 57999-60 red)
- 40277-55A compensating sprocket (in place of rigid)

Harley gave the Duo-Glide yet another styling update for 1960, as shown here on this FL restored by Elmer Ehnes.

Tank emblems were the same as those of 1959, but revised tank paneling updated the overall look for the new decade.

- 63587-58 rear chain oiler
- 49150-58 chrome rear safety guard
- frame-mounted buddy seat (choice of 52485-60 black and white, 52481-60 red and white, and 52489-60 all white)

Road Cruiser Group F-2A was the same as F-2 but with a pair of black plastic saddlebags instead of white.

Road Cruiser Group F-3 was same as F-2 but with a deluxe solo saddle in place of the frame-mounted buddy seat. Road Cruiser Group F-3A was the same as F-3 but with a pair of black saddlebags instead of white.

Road Cruiser Group F-4 was also the same as F-2 except that the super deluxe buddy seat was substituted for the frame-mounted buddy seat. Road Cruiser Group F-4A was the same as F-4 but with 90851-58A black plastic saddlebags instead of white.

King of the Highway Group F-5 was the deluxe touring package. It included:

- 66373-54 chrome battery cover
- 90849-58 pair of white plastic saddle bags and carrier
- windshield (choice of 57996-60 clear, 57998-60 blue, or 57999-60 red)
- 63587-58 rear chain oiler
- 40277-55A compensating sprocket (in place of rigid)
- 65425-58 dual mufflers with crossover
- 68550-58 directional signals (partially attached)
- 65700-38 chrome boot guard
- 49150-58 chrome rear safety guard
- 53403-58 chrome luggage carrier (not attached)
- 91075-58A front bumper (not attached) and 91007-58 rear bumper (not attached)
- 43895-56 chrome axle and fork studs (attached)
- 43303-49 front hub cap (attached)
- 59887-59 rear fender tip
- frame-mounted buddy seat (choice of 52485-60 black and white, 52487-60 red and white, 52489-60 all white)

Group F-5A was the same as F-5 except that it included black plastic saddlebags instead of white.

King of the Highway Group F-6 was the deluxe touring package for solo riders, substituting the deluxe solo seat for the frame-mounted buddy seat. Group F-6A was the same as F-6 except with black plastic saddlebags instead of white.

King of the Highway Group F-7 was the same as F-5, but substituted the super deluxe buddy seat for the frame-mounted buddy seat. Group F-7A was the same as F-7 except black plastic saddlebags were substituted for white.

The Standard Police Group FP-1 included:

- front-wheel siren
- speedometer hand control (attached)
- deluxe solo saddle (exchange)
- oil filter

Group FP-2 also included a foot control for the siren. Group FP-3 substituted a foot-controlled rear-wheel siren for the hand-controlled front-wheel siren.

Factory Paint Options

A new two-tone gas-tank scheme was used with the arrow tank emblems for 1960. The scheme consisted of a tank's paint schemecolored top and white side panels with a colored stripe curving from front to back underneath the tank emblems. Fenders were painted in the tank color, without panels.

Two standard color combinations were offered: Skyline Blue with Birch White tank side panels or Black with Birch White tank side panels. Optional (at extra cost) were Hi-Fi Blue with Birch White tank side panels, Hi-Fi Red with Birch White tank side panels, or Hi-Fi Green with Birch White tank side panels. Police Silver (Police Group only), Birch White (Police Group only), or any standard color without tank panels were also available for no additional cost.

New fork covers formed a massive-looking nacelle around the headlight for 1960.

The smooth style of primary cover was used through the end of the Duo-Glide line in 1964.

In stripped form with a solo seat and the narrow Speedster handlebars, the Duo-Glide remained a relatively svelte machine.

With bags, buddy seat, and windshield, the Duo-Glide was transformed into the most massive of 1960s touring machines. This one carries the restyled buddy seat for 1961. It was also available in a frame-mounted (non-sprung) version.

Chassis Updates and Detail Changes

For 1960, the Hydra-Glide forks were given a whole new look. Gone were the front fork covers with the three V stripes and the separate headlight, replaced by a two-piece nacelle that covered the front of the fork and enclosed the headlight for a more massive but streamlined appearance.

The shroud pieces were stamped aluminum, either polished or not (unpolished shrouds were sometimes painted black). This style of nacelle was used through the end of the FLH line in 1984 and was resurrected 10 years later on Harley's popular Road King models.

Changes to the front end were more than nacelle-deep, however. The forks were fitted with new top fork brackets, handlebars, handlebar risers, and riser covers. Two types of top fork brackets were introduced, one for adjustable-rake forks and another for non-adjustable forks. The new brackets were necessary to accommodate the new bars and risers and were used through 1964.

The new handlebars were two-piece bars with a separate bar for each side. As in previous years, Buckhorn or Speedster handlebars were offered, and all had threaded outside ends for the ⅜-inch end screws that retained the control spirals (these are the same spirals that had been used since 1954). Solid-mounted bars were black; optional rubber-mounted bars were chromed.

The 1960 speedometer was the same as the 1958 model. This speedometer would be used through 1961.

Handlebars were an all-new two-piece (left and right) design for 1960. The bars are mounted to the fork by a center clamp that replaces the riser.

This 1960 Duo-Glide is fitted with earlier-style leather buddy seat and bags. That year, Harley offered only hard bags and more modern-looking frame and spring-mounted buddy seats in all white, black and white, or red and white.

The only substantial change inside the Panhead motor for 1960 was the midyear switch to FLH-type stellite-faced valves on the FL models.

The separate bars are clamped in the center by the handlebar clamp, which is bolted to the fork top bracket. This clamp takes the place of the risers that had been used since 1949. On rubber-mounted bars, the clamps featured rubber bushings to isolate the bars from engine vibration. These two-piece bars are correct for 1960–1964 Duo-Glides.

Handlebar clamps were covered by a large aluminum cover. Standard covers were unpolished aluminum, but polished covers were optional. If a steering damper was fitted (H-D recommended the steering damper only for use with a sidecar), the handlebar cover was drilled with a large hole for the steering-damper-shaft knob. This style of handlebar cover is correct for 1960–1965.

Brackets and lower panels for the optional windshields were redesigned to fit the new headlight nacelle. The new windshield assembly was used through 1965. The mounts for the optional spot lamps were also redesigned to work with the new nacelle (the lamps themselves are the same). The new lamp assemblies were also used through 1965.

The top-of-the-line option group in 1960 was the King of the Highway Group, which included a windshield, compensating sprocket, dual exhaust, chrome front and rear safety guards, white or black saddle bags, and choice of Frame-Mounted Buddy Seat, Deluxe Solo Saddle, or Super Deluxe Buddy Seat. This bike is fitted with the correct style of post-mounted black and white Super Deluxe Buddy Seat, which was offered in all white, red and white, and in black and white.

Frame-Mounted Seats New for 1960, the frame-mounted buddy seats that were part of the Road Cruiser and King of the Highway packages (and also available for order separately) modernized the Duo-Glide's look as much as the new headlight nacelles did. The new seat was offered in all white, black and white, and red and white. These frame-mounted seats were offered through 1965.

Base-model Duo-Glides still came with the old post-mounted solo seat, and deluxe and buddy versions of the post seat were also still available for 1960. The optional Super Deluxe Buddy Seat was completely redesigned to give a more modern look. The new seat featured a vinyl top covering, vinyl side covering, and leather skirt. The seat was offered in all white; red top, white side, and white skirt; or black top, white side, and white skirt. These seats were offered for 1960–1964.

Rear Brake Drum A new rear brake drum was fitted for 1960. The main difference between this and the drum it replaced was that the drive sprocket was riveted to the new hub with ³/₁₆-inch rivets (rather than ⅛-inch rivets). This new hub featured the number "41409-48A" cast in relief on the hub side. It was fitted through 1962.

Motor Updates

In mid-1960, the stellite-faced exhaust valves that had been fitted to the FLH since mid-1958 were finally fitted to FL models as well. These valves were fitted to all FL and FLH models through 1965.

Many bright bits from the Chrome Finish Group are shown here, including the chrome rim, muffler, and caps for the shock absorbers.

Harley gave the Duo-Glide yet another new look for 1961, with a new two-tone tank pattern and new emblems. This one was restored by Bob Bowes.

Harley abandoned its tried-and-true "wasted-spark" ignition for 1961. Instead of one coil and one set of points firing both cylinders, the 1961 Duo-Glides had twin points and coils, each firing a separate cylinder.

Production for 1960

Sales for 1960 were up slightly from the previous year, at 5,967. Harley-Davidson documents do not show how many of each model were sold. Even though it was by far the most expensive bike in the lineup, the Duo-Glide was Harley's best seller by far, outselling even the new Topper scooter.

The 1961 Duo-Glides

For 1961, Harley's stylists gave the Duo-Glide another facelift with new star tank emblems and restyled two-tone paint, and Harley's engineers gave the engine a new ignition that used twin points and coils to time and fire each cylinder individually—"single-fire" ignition, as it's called today.

Models, Prices, and Option Groups

The 1961 Duo-Glides were available with the FL and FLH engines. Each motor was available with hand shift (designated Model FL or FLH) or foot shift (designated Model FLF or FLHF). Per usual H-D practice, only FL or FLH, not the "F" for "foot shift," was stamped into the case as part of the serial number. Police or sidecar gearing was also available as a no-cost option.

Base-model 1961 FLH Duo-Glides retailed for $1,400, and base-model FL Duo-Glides retailed for $1,335, both $25 higher than the previous

year. Base models were equipped with a black front safety guard, an air cleaner, a jiffy stand, and black wheels with 5.00x16-inch tires, but nine solo and three police option groups were offered to dress up the basic bike.

The Chrome Finish Group F-1 was a package including all the most popular dress-up accessories:

* 49038-58 chrome front safety guard
* chrome rubber-mounted handlebars (choice of speedster or buckhorn)
* 43007-40 chrome rims
* 45964-49 stainless-steel fork covers
* 60557-36 chrome clutch-inspection cover
* 32589-36 chrome timer cover
* 60573-36 chrome primary-chain-inspection cover
* 65203-58 chrome muffler
* polished fork sliders
* 44141-50 polished brake side cover
* 69022-54 chrome horn cover
* 69140-54 chrome horn trumpet
* 65550-58 chrome exhaust-pipe covers
* colored plastic handlebar grips
* 71271-56 chrome instrument-panel cover
* 63800-58 oil filter
* 54704-60 chrome caps for rear shock absorber
* 38495-58 chrome clutch booster-spring cover
* polished headlamp nacelle and handlebar-clamp cover
* 31800-61 chrome spark-coil cover

The new twin coils mount to the frame, just forward of the oil tank.

This new style of FLH decal appeared for 1961. It was applied to both sides of the oil tank on 1961–1964 FLHs.

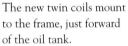

These new "star" emblems were standard for 1961 and 1962.

Also new for 1961 was the generator, which was redesigned so that it required less maintenance.

These Royalite plastic saddlebags were optional on 1957 to 1962 Panheads.

The year 1961 was the last year for this style of dash and speedometer.

The Road Cruiser Group F-2 was a package of the basic touring accessories. It included:

- 91007-58 chrome rear bumper
- 91075-58A chrome front bumper
- 90849-59 white plastic saddlebags and carrier
- windshield (choice of 57996-60 clear, 57998-60 blue, or 57999-60 red)
- 40277-60 compensating sprocket (in place of rigid)
- 63587-58 rear-chain oiler (attached), and
- Super Deluxe Buddy Seat (choice of 52504-58A black and white or 52505-58 red and white).

Road Cruiser Group F-2A was the same as F-2 but with black plastic saddlebags instead of white.

Road Cruiser Group F-3 was the same as F-2 but with a frame-mounted buddy seat in place of the Super Deluxe buddy seat. The seat was available in black-and-white, red-and-white, and all-white versions.

Road Cruiser Group F-4 was also the same as F-2 but substituted the deluxe solo seat for the super deluxe buddy seat.

The King of the Highway Group F-5 was the deluxe touring package. It included:

- 66373-54 chrome battery cover
- 90849-58 white plastic saddlebags and carrier
- windshield (choice of 57996-60 clear, 57998-60 blue, or 57999-60 red)
- 63587-58 rear-chain oiler
- 40277-60 compensating sprocket (in place of rigid)
- 65425-58 dual mufflers with crossover
- 68550-58B directional signals (partially attached)
- 65700-38 chrome boot guard
- 49150-58 chrome rear safety guard
- 53403-58 chrome luggage carrier (not attached)
- 91075-58A chrome front bumper (not attached)
- 91007-58 chrome rear bumper (not attached)
- 43895-56 chrome axle and fork stud caps (attached)
- 43303-49 front hub cap (attached)
- 59887-59 chrome rear fender tip, and
- Super Deluxe Buddy Seat (52504-58A black and white, or 52505-58 red and white)

Group F-5A was the same as F-5 except that it included black plastic saddlebags instead of white.

King of the Highway Group F-6 was the same as F-5 except that the frame-mounted buddy seat replaced the super deluxe buddy seat.

King of the Highway Group F-7 was the deluxe touring package for solo riders, substituting the deluxe solo seat for the super deluxe buddy seat.

The Standard Police Group FP-1 included:

- front-wheel siren
- speedometer hand control (attached)
- deluxe solo saddle (exchange)
- oil filter

Fishtail mufflers first became an option for 1961.

Group FP-2 also included a foot control for the siren. Group FP-3 substituted a foot-controlled rear-wheel siren for the hand-controlled front-wheel siren.

Factory Paint Options

Gas tanks were given new "star" tank emblems and two-tone paint schemes for 1961. Standard color combinations were Pepper Red with Birch White tank side stripes, and Black with Birch White tank side stripes. Fenders were painted in the tank color, without panels.

Optional were Hi-Fi Blue with Birch White tank side stripes, Hi-Fi Red with Birch White tank side stripes, Hi-Fi Green with Birch White tank side stripes, Police Silver (Police Group only), Birch White (Police Group only), and any standard color solid (without tank panels).

Chassis Updates and Detail Changes

All the chassis updates for 1961 were cosmetic. These included the aforementioned new tank emblems and two-tone paint schemes, as well as a new style of FLH decal. The new decal featured a large red stylized H (its shape suggests that of a lightning bolt) on a white field, framed by checkered stripes above and below. This decal should be applied to both sides of the oil tank on all 1961–1964 FLHs.

Motor Updates

Changes to the engine for 1961 were also relatively minor, including the switch to what is known today as a "single-fire" ignition, revised pushrods, a new generator, and a new-style dual exhaust.

Dual-Point Ignition Since before the days of the Knucklehead, Harley Big Twins had been fitted with a single-point timer and a twin-lead coil that fires both spark plugs every time the points opened—called the "wasted-spark" system. For 1961, the entire ignition system (timer, points, condenser, and coil) was changed to use separate primary and secondary ignition circuits for each cylinder. The result is that each spark plug fires separately.

Instead of one set of contact points and a two-lobed points cam, the new timer used two sets of contact points and a new single-lobe cam. It also carried a separate condenser for each set of points. As on the earlier timer, ignition advance was controlled manually by twisting the spiral on the left handlebar. The timer body and cover were cadmium plated (chrome-plated covers were optional), and the timer was driven at half-speed by a gear in the gear case. The dual-point timer was fitted from 1961 to 1964.

Instead of a single square-section coil with twin leads, the new system used twin round-section single-lead coils. The new coils had no

A new tank-striping scheme gave the 1962 bikes a unique identity. This 1962 Fl was restored by John Viljoen and Scott Lange.

integral mounting lugs, so the two coils were fastened together at the bottom by a connector and then were bolted to a bracket by a mounting plate and bolt. This bracket mounted to the frame on the left side, just forward of the oil tank. The coils were usually covered by the optional chrome-plated cover.

In theory, single-fire ignition allows more precise tuning of the engine and provides a smoother idle. In practice, however, these advantages were outweighed by the more complicated maintenance.

That was especially true on the early-1961 Duo-Glides (prior to 61FLH7987), which were assembled with the same left flywheels that had been used on motors with the earlier, single-point timers. These flywheels only have a timing mark for the front cylinder, since this was all that was necessary to time the single-point ignition. To properly time these motors, the tuner had to use a special Harley-Davidson timing gauge that was screwed into the rear cylinder's spark-plug hole to sense the piston position. Motors numbered 61FLH7987 and higher were fitted with a new left flywheel with a timing mark for the rear cylinder.

Pushrods Inside the motor, new pushrods were fitted that differed slightly in design from the old rods. The main body section of the new rod was

longer than the body of the old rod, but the pressed-in bottom piece on the new rod was much shorter, so the overall length of the two rods was the same: 8 $\frac{13}{16}$ inches. This new rod was fitted to 1961–1965 motors.

Model 61 Generator In the never-ending quest to make its Duo-Glide more maintenance-free, Harley-Davidson fitted an updated generator with bearings that did not require frequent greasing.

Like the Model 58 generator it replaced, the new Model 61 generator was a two-brush, 6-volt generator used with an external voltage regulator mounted alongside the rear cylinder on the left side. This generator was fitted to 1961–1964 civilian Duo-Glides. Radio-equipped Duo-Glides for these years used the same Model 51 radio generator that had been used since 1952.

Dual Exhaust The optional dual-exhaust systems fitted to Panheads through early 1961 were, in effect, twin single-exhaust systems. On these systems, the left muffler was connected by a combination left-rear/rear-header pipe to the rear cylinder only, and the right muffler connected via the front header pipe, S-pipe, and right dual-exhaust pipe to the front cylinder only.

On the new system, introduced during the 1961 sales season, a new rear header pipe and left rear pipe connected the exhaust from the front and rear cylinders together to feed both mufflers. The new system used the front header, S-pipe, the Y-pipe used on the single-exhaust system, plus a new rear header pipe that connected to the Y-pipe and had an integral connection for a new left-rear pipe. This new left-rear pipe snaked around behind the engine and back to the rear muffler. S-pipe, Y-pipe, rear header, and left rear pipes were chrome plated.

Standard mufflers on the dual system were the short, tubular mufflers that had been fitted since 1958 (optional "fishtail" mufflers were introduced in late 1961). The new intercon-nected dual exhaust is correct for mid-1961–1964 Panheads. Also optional for late 1961 and later exhaust systems was a new chromed exhaust-pipe guard that clamped to the bend of the front header pipe.

Production for 1961

Duo-Glide production bottomed out once again during 1961 to 4,927 units, 17 percent fewer than the previous year. Hondas were being sold by the tens of thousands, and Harley-Davidson's sales were suffering.

The 1962 Duo-Glides

As sales for the Big Twin languished, Harley-Davidson seemed less inclined to spend any money updating them. Except for an internally revised oil pump introduced in midyear, only cosmetic changes were made in 1962.

The most prominent of these is the new paint job for the gas tanks. The tanks were given new racing stripes that sweep back and taper from the instrument cover to the rear end of the tank. The star tank emblem that had been introduced in 1961 was used again on these tanks.

Models, Prices, and Option Groups

The 1962 Duo-Glides were available with the FL and FLH engines. Each motor was available with hand shift (FL or FLH) or foot shift (FLF or FLHF). Per usual H-D practice, only FL or FLH, not the "F" for "foot shift," was stamped into the case as part of the serial number. Police or sidecar gearing was also available as a no-cost option.

Base-model 1962 FLH Duo-Glides retailed for $1,400, and base-model FL Duo-Glides for $1,335, both the same as the previous year. Base models were equipped with a black front safety guard, an air cleaner, a jiffy stand, and black wheels with 5.00x16-inch tires, but seven solo option groups and one police option group were offered to dress up the basic bike.

Star tank badges were reprised for 1962.

This revised dash and speedometer were introduced for 1962.

The 1962 models retained the dual-coil ignition introduced in 1961. The coils on this machine are hidden behind a chrome cover that was included with the Chrome Finish Group.

The new tank stripes gave the 1962 Duo-Glides a muscular look.

Many rear-end parts shown here were used for the last time in 1962, including the chain guard, brake backing plate, and turn signals.

One thing never changed during the Panhead years: Owners wanted to dress up their bikes with lots of chrome, and Harley-Davidson did its best to supply it.

The Chrome Finish Group F-1 was a package of all the most popular dress-up accessories. It included the following items:

- chrome clutch booster-spring cover, clutch cover, exhaust-pipe cover, front safety guard, horn trumpet and cover, primary-chain-inspection cover, instrument-panel cover, mirror, muffler, oil filter, rims, shock-absorber caps, spark-coil cover, and timer cover
- rubber-mounted chrome handlebars (choice of Speedster or Buckhorn)
- polished brake side cover, fork sliders, handle-bar-clamp cover, and headlamp nacelle
- stainless-steel fork covers

The Road Cruiser Group F-2 was a package of the basic touring accessories. It included:

- chrome front and rear bumpers
- white plastic saddlebags and carrier
- solo windshield (choice of clear, red, or blue)
- compensating sprocket
- rear-chain oiler
- Super Deluxe buddy seat (black and white, red and white, or all white)

Road Cruiser Group F-3 was same as F-2 but with a frame-mounted buddy seat in place of the Super Deluxe buddy seat. The seat was available in black-and-white, red-and-white, and all-white versions.

Road Cruiser Group F-4 was also the same as F-2 but substituted the deluxe solo seat for the super deluxe buddy seat.

The King of the Highway Group F-5 was the deluxe touring package. It included
- chrome axle and fork-stud cap, battery cover, boot guards, front bumper, rear bumper, rear-fender tip, dual mufflers (super quiet, but standard dual mufflers could be substituted at no extra charge), luggage carrier, and rear safety guard
- compensating sprocket
- front hub cap
- directional signals
- white plastic saddle-bags
- rear-chain oiler
- solo windshield (choice of blue, clear, or red)
- Super Deluxe buddy seat (choice of red and white, black and white, or all white)

King of the Highway Group F-6 was the same as F-5 with the frame-mounted buddy seat replacing the super deluxe buddy seat.

King of the Highway Group F-7 was the deluxe touring package for solo riders, substituting the deluxe solo seat for the super deluxe buddy seat.

Front-wheel sirens were not offered for 1962, so Police Groups FP-1 and FP-2 were discontinued. Group FP-3 was offered, and included:
- deluxe solo seat
- foot-controlled rear-wheel siren
- oil filter
- rear-chain oiler
- clear solo windshield
- special police speedometer
- speedometer hand control

Factory Paint Options
The 1962 Duo-Glides were offered in two standard color combinations: Tango Red tank with Birch White side stripes and Black tank with Birch White side stripes. Optional were Hi-Fi Blue tank with Birch White side stripes, Hi-Fi Red tank with Birch White side stripes, Hi-Fi Purple tank with Birch White side stripes, Police Silver (Police Group only), and Birch White (Police Group only). Optional were Hi-Fi Blue with White tank side stripes, Hi-Fi Red with White tank side stripes, and Hi-Fi Purple with White tank side stripes. Fenders were painted in the tank color, without panels.

Chassis Updates and Detail Changes
Chassis updates for 1962 were all cosmetic and included an updated look for the speedometer, instrument cover, and optional front spotlight.

Speedometer The Stewart-Warner speedometer was given yet another facelift for 1962. This speedometer featured a flat, single-level face with

Above: By the early 1960s when this FL was built, almost the entire production was of foot-shift Duo-Glides like this one.

These handlebar grips were new for 1962. Harley-Davidson continued using them into the 1970s.

a center panel shaped like a tombstone. The name "Harley-Davidson" was painted in black on the aluminum, just to the rear of the trip meter. Mile-per-hour numbers (1 through 12), hash marks for the 10s, and dots for the intermediate 2-mile-per-hour increments were bare brushed aluminum out of the black-painted outer face of the speedometer. The odometer and trip-meter miles numerals were white on a black background, and the trip-meter tenth-mile numerals were black on a white background. This style of speedometer is correct for 1962–1965 Panheads.

The 1962 Duo-Glide engines were the last to route oil through passages in the cylinders to the cylinder heads.

Instrument Cover The new speedometer was housed in a new instrument cover. The new cover was similar to the previous dash, except that the rectangular center GEN/OIL lens was replaced by three (two, on hand-shift bikes) separate, round indicator-lens covers. The left (red) lens covered the generator light, the center (green) lens covered the neutral light, and the right (also red) lens covered the oil-pressure light. On hand-shift bikes, the center indicator (neutral) light was omitted. As was true for the previous instrument covers, standard covers were painted the color of the tank, and chrome-plated covers were optional. This instrument cover is correct for 1962–1965 Panheads.

Front Spot Lights Also for 1962, the optional front spot lights were given new housings with shallower, more rounded backs. New brackets were introduced to mount these new lamps to the forks. These lamps and mounts are correct for 1962–1965.

Production for 1962 Harley-Davidson production was up slightly in 1962, to 10,497 units, of which 5,184 were Duo-Glides. Meanwhile, business

was booming for the foreign competition. Triumph's sales were up over 20,000 units, but the biggest competitor was Honda, which was selling as many motorcycles as all other makers combined. Honda was gradually introducing larger models, and other Japanese makers—including Kawasaki, Suzuki, and Yamaha—were making their mark.

The 1963 Duo-Glides

For 1963, Harley-Davidson's designers gave the Duo-Glide a subtle restyle and made extensive modifications to the engine to reroute the oil path to the cylinder heads through external oil lines.

Models, Prices, and Option Groups

For 1963, the Duo-Glide was again offered in two basic models—FL and FLH—and in foot-shift or hand-shift versions of each, with sidecar or police gearing optional. The FLHs retailed for $1,425, and the FL machines for $1,360, each $25 more than the previous year.

The 1963 Duo-Glides were available with the FL and FLH engines. Each motor was available with hand shift (FL or FLH) or foot shift (FLF or FLHF). Per usual H-D practice, only FL or FLH, not the "F" for "foot shift," was stamped into the case as part of the serial number. Police or sidecar gearing was also available as a no-cost option.

Base-model 1963 FLH Duo-Glides retailed for $1,425, and base-model FL Duo-Glides for $1,360, both $25 more than the previous year. Base models were equipped with a black front safety guard, an air cleaner, a jiffy stand, rear-chain oiler, and black wheels with 5.00x16-inch tires, but four solo and two police option groups were offered to dress up the basic bike.

The Chrome Finish Group F-1 was a package of all the most popular dress-up accessories. It included the following items:

- chrome clutch booster-spring cover, clutch-inspection cover, exhaust-pipe covers, front safety guard, horn trumpet and cover, primary-chain inspection cover, instrument panel, mirror, muffler, rims, shock-absorber covers, spark-coil cover, and timer cover
- oil filter (attached)
- polished brake side cover, fork sliders, handlebar cover, and headlamp nacelle
- chrome rubber-mounted handlebars (choice of Speedster or Buckhorn)
- stainless-steel fork covers

The King of the Highway Group F-5 was the deluxe touring package. It included:

- chrome axle and fork-stud caps (attached), battery cover, boot guard, front and rear bumper, rear-fender tip, luggage carrier, rear safety guard, and oil tank

- dual chrome super-quiet mufflers
- compensating sprocket
- front hub cap (attached)
- directional signals
- white fiberglass saddlebags and carrier
- solo windshield (choice of blue, clear, or red)
- super deluxe buddy seat (choice of red and white, black and white, or all white)

Optional for all King of the Highway Groups: Standard dual mufflers 65425-61 may be substituted for the super quiet mufflers, and black fiberglass saddlebags and carrier may be substituted for white at no extra charge.

King of the Highway Group F-6 was the same as F-5 with the frame-mounted buddy seat replacing the super deluxe buddy seat.

King of the Highway Group F-7 was the deluxe touring package for solo riders, substituting the deluxe solo seat for the super deluxe buddy seat.

Standard Police Group FP-1 included:

- deluxe solo seat
- foot-controlled rear-wheel siren
- oil filter
- clear solo windshield
- special police speedometer
- speedometer hand control

Police Group FP-2 is the same as FP-1 but also includes a hand control for the siren.

Factory Paint Options

The two-tone paint scheme on the tank was changed once again for 1963. The tank had racing stripes as in 1962, but for 1963 the stripes swept back along the top of the tank rather than down along the sides of the tank. Fenders were painted in the tank color, without panels.

Three standard color combinations were offered: Tango Red with white tank stripes, Horizon Metallic Blue with white tank stripes, and Black with white tank stripes. Optional were Hi-Fi Turquoise with white tank stripes, Hi-Fi Red with white tank stripes, Hi-Fi Purple with white tank stripes, Police Silver (Police Group only), and Birch White (Police Group only).

Chassis Updates and Detail Changes

The Duo-Glide chassis was updated for 1963 with new-style paint and tank badges, better brakes, and restyled starter pedal, chain guard, turn signals, and saddlebags.

Braking Power More-powerful rear brakes were fitted for 1963. The new brake hub looked just like previous hubs, except that it was deeper (2⅛ inches instead of 1⅞ inches) to allow use of wider brake shoes (1¹³⁄₁₆ inches instead of 1⁵⁄₁₆ inches) and lacked the dust lip that had been cast into previous hubs. This hub is correct for 1963–1965 Panheads.

A new backing plate was introduced to go with the new hub and shoes. This backing plate was 8⅝ inches in diameter (the old plate was 8⅛ inches) and has a rolled lip around the edge to replace the dust lip that was deleted on the hub. It also featured a reinforcement plate attached by four rivets to the outside of the brake backing plate, covering the wheel-cylinder mounting area to below the mounting stud. The hub and backing plate were painted black. These rear brake hubs, shoes, and backing plates were used on 1963–1965 Panheads.

"Bar-and-Shield" Tank Emblems New tank emblems graced the tanks of 1963 Duo-Glides, stamped in the shape of the Harley-Davidson bar-and-shield trademark. The elongated bar had the company name stamped into it. This emblem is correct on 1963–1965 Panheads.

"Fudge-Sickle" Starter Pedal The bicycle-pedal style of kick-starter pedal was replaced with a one-piece "fudge-sickle" style starter pedal for 1963. Standard pedals were molded of black rubber, but white pedals were available as an option. The one-piece pedal is correct for 1963–1965 Panheads.

Valanced Chain Guard The drive-chain guard was revised slightly for 1963—much more deeply valanced than its predecessor with its rear tip flared back. The guard also featured an embossed oval to provide clearance for the brake-line swivel fitting that protrudes from the brake backing plate.

Turn Signals The venerable bullet-shaped lamps that had been used for the front and rear parking lights and turn signals were replaced with round-back lamps and new mounts for 1963. The front lamps have amber lenses and mount to the sides of the forks, and the rear lamps have red or amber lenses and mount to a chromed bracket that wraps around the taillight. These lamps are correct for 1963–1965.

Fiberglass Saddlebags New fiberglass saddlebags replaced the optional Royalite plastic bags for 1963. These bags mounted to their carriers with two latches and a spring clip and had a rubber molding stapled to the top rim of the bags to seal the cover. They were available in black or white and are the correct bags for 1963 Panheads.

Motor Updates

The biggest change for 1963 was that Harley-Davidson engineers extensively modified the Panhead engine, routing oil to the heads through external oil lines. This system had been used on

Duo-Glides for 1963 were restyled with new tank emblems, striping, and gear cover. They also were fitted with a revised oiling system that routed oil to the heads through external oil pipes.

all Knucklehead motors but was abandoned for the first Panhead motor.

Why the change back? Two possible explanations come to mind. First, oil routed through an external line would arrive at the head at a cooler temperature than oil routed through a passage in the hot cylinder casting. Second, an oil line with two fittings is easier to seal than are the two gasket surfaces—above and below the cylinder—that each internal oil passage must go through.

A boss for the external oil line was added to the right crankcase, placed to the right of the "peak" created in the case at the point where the tappet blocks meet. Oil was routed to the boss through a hollow bolt from oil passages in the redesigned gear case. This right crankcase and gear cover were used in 1963 and 1964. The left case was not revised.

New cylinders were introduced that no longer had the oil passages on the right side of the casting. These cylinder castings still had the oil-return passage in the left side of the casting and were painted silver. These new cylinders were used from 1963–1965.

Also part of the system were new cylinder heads that had a drilled and threaded boss

between the lowest two fins on the right side, near the intake port. The oil line from the crankcase branched off and attached to the boss on each head, and a passage from the boss fed oil to the rocker passages in the heads. Outside-oiler heads were used from 1963–1965.

Production for 1963
Panhead sales reached an all-time low of 4,300 during 1963. Overall sales were just as poor, off by over 11 percent. Harley-Davidson sold just 9,873 motorcycles, the smallest total sales since 1940.

The 1964 Duo-Glides

Busy working on the Duo-Glide's replacement, Harley-Davidson engineers made only minimal changes to the Duo-Glide for its last year. As in previous years, though, they did change the paint scheme, giving the last-year Duo-Glide its own unique identity.

Models, Prices, and Option Groups
The 1964 Duo-Glides were available with the FL

Super Solo and FLH Super Sport engines. Each motor was available with hand shift (FL or FLH) or foot shift (FLF or FLHF). Per usual H-D practice, only FL or FLH, not the "F" for "foot shift," was stamped into the case as part of the serial number. Police or sidecar gearing was also available as a no-cost option.

Base-model 1964 FLH Duo-Glides retailed for $1,450, and base-model FL Duo-Glides for $1,385, both $25 more than the previous year. Base models were equipped with a black front safety guard, an air cleaner, a jiffy stand, rear-chain oiler, and black wheels with 5.00x16-inch tires, but four solo and two police option groups were offered to dress up the basic bike.

The Chrome Finish Group F-1 was a package of all the most popular dress-up accessories. It included the following items:
- chrome clutch booster-spring cover, clutch cover, exhaust-pipe covers, front safety guard, horn trumpet and cover, inspection cover, instrument panel, mirror, muffler, rims, shock absorber covers, spark-coil cover, and timer cover
- oil filter (attached)

- polished brake side cover, fork sliders, handlebar cover, and headlamp nacelle
- rubber-mounted chrome handlebars (speedster or buckhorn)
- stainless-steel fork covers

The King of the Highway Group F-5 was the deluxe touring package. It included:
- chrome axle and fork stud cover (attached), battery cover, boot guard, front and rear bumper,

For its last year, the duo-Glide got yet another facelift. This 1964 Duo-Glide was restored by Gene Schrier. Gene restores his machines to the standard of "How Harley would build them today." That means no Parkerized or cad-plated parts—chrome instead.

The new tank panels look especially striking when paired with whitewall tires.

Both civilian and police bikes for 1964 kept the bar-and-shield tank emblems introduced in 1963.

rear-fender tip, dual super-quiet mufflers, luggage carrier, rear safety guard, and oil tank
- compensating sprocket
- front hub cap (attached)
- directional signals
- white fiberglass saddlebags
- solo windshield (choice of: blue, clear or red)
- super deluxe buddy seat (choice of red and white, black and white, or all white)

Radio-equipped police bikes were fitted with a higher-output generator and larger regulator, as shown here.

Optional for all King of the Highway Groups: "Normal-tone" dual mufflers 65425-61 could be substituted for the super-quiet mufflers, and black fiberglass saddlebags and carrier could be substituted for white at no extra charge.

King of the Highway Group F-6 was the same as F-5 except the frame-mounted buddy seat replaced the super deluxe buddy seat.

King of the Highway Group F-7 was the deluxe touring package for solo riders, substituting the deluxe solo seat for the super deluxe buddy seat.

Standard Police Group FP-1 included:
- deluxe solo seat
- foot-controlled rear-wheel siren
- oil filter
- clear solo windshield
- special police speedometer
- speedometer hand control

Police Group FP-2 was the same as FP-1 but also included a hand-control for the siren.

Factory Paint Options

The two-tone paint scheme on the tank was changed once again for 1964. The racing stripes

Instead of polished forks, those of the police bikes were usually painted black.

gave way to broad white side panels. The Panheads were offered in two standard color combinations, Fiesta Red with white tank panels and Black with white tank stripes. Optional were Hi-Fi Blue with white tank stripes, Hi-Fi Red with white tank panels, Police Silver (Police Group only), and Birch White (Police Group only). Fenders were painted in the tank color, without panels.

Chassis Updates and Detail Changes

Other than the tank paneling, only a few other details changed on both the chassis and the motor for 1964.

The inner primary-chain housing was slightly revised, with a new position for the breather-pipe hole. This inner guard was used for 1964 only.

In late 1964, an optional two-part (upper and lower) chrome-plated rear-chain guard was introduced. It was also optional for 1965.

Shown in this view are the calibrated police speedometer and radio speaker and handset.

Civilian bikes were graced with new tank panels that really dressed up the last Duo-Glides.

The friction-type siren gets its power from the rear wheel. It is engaged by the heel lever shown at the left of the photo.

The optional fiberglass saddlebags were also slightly redesigned in 1964. The rubber sealing strip that was stapled on the upper rim of the earlier bags was replaced by weather stripping glued around the cover's edge.

Production for 1964

Harley-Davidson's sales surged by 34 percent for 1964, mostly from sales of Duo-Glides and Sportsters. Big Twin sales rose from 4,300 in 1963 to 5,500 in 1964, while sales of Sprints and other small bikes were flat.

Why the sudden change in Harley's fortunes? Possibly because the war babies and baby boomers reached early adulthood. Possibly because the economy was strong. Possibly because leisure time was increasing for Americans at all social levels, and many had more disposable income to spend on their leisure activities. Most likely, it was the cumulative impact of all these factors. Whatever the reason, Harley-Davidson and all the other motorcycle makers experienced record sales for the next several years.

Chapter 4

The 1965
Electra Glides

Even as late as the mid-1960s, Harley-Davidson still considered its FLH the company "hot rod." Everyone else knew that Harley's Big Twin had long ago lost the performance war to the smaller Sportster and to British sportsters such as the Triumph Bonneville and Norton Dominator. Worse yet, Harley's Big Twin began losing yet another skirmish, in the early 1960s, to a new foe. That skirmish? The "Push Button Wars." The foe? Honda, and soon a slew of other Japanese companies.

In the early 1960s, Harley-Davidson was selling about 10,000 motorcycles a year to hard-core enthusiasts. Upstart Honda, on the other hand, had been in the U.S. market just a few years, yet it was selling bigger and bigger motorcycles by the hundreds of thousands every year to mainstream Americans.

For 1965, Harley-Davidson so changed its big twin that it was almost a new machine. This Electra Glide in the optional Hi-Fi Blue and white combination was restored by Jerry Richards.

The main stimulus for all the changes was the addition of electric start. This Electra Glide was restored by Eugene Schrier. As mentioned previously, he restores his bikes to a "How Harley would build them today" standard, which means lots of extra chrome. It was painted in Hi-Fi Turquoise and white, which was not a standard combination for 1965.

Harley called the updated big twin "Electra Glide," as announced by the chrome emblems on each side of the front fender.

Sure, there was a huge price difference between Hondas and Harleys, but that doesn't really explain the even huger disparity in sales figures. What really distinguished the Honda from the Harley in the eyes of the general public was much simpler: If you wanted to ride your Honda, all you had to do was turn the key and push the start button, but if you wanted to ride your Harley, you had to go through an arcane starting ritual that looked to the uninitiated like equal parts exercise and exorcism. Soichiro Honda's genius was in realizing that motorcycles would never appeal to the masses until they were just as easy to start and as reliable as a car, and then making it happen.

Harley-Davidson caught the push-button vibe for 1965. Outwardly, the 1965 Harley Big Twins looked a little pudgier, but not all that different from the 1964 Duo-Glides. That's because the good stuff was hidden from view behind new covers and cases. Chrome script on each side of the front fender, however, gave name to Harley's new era in a dialect all Motor Company fans were sure to understand: Electra Glide. That's "Electra" as in electric start. More than anything Harley-Davidson had ever done, this change had a cultural impact.

How's that?

Well, kick-starting had always been an honored rite of passage among Big Twin riders. The standard answer to a son's/little brother's/nephew's/neighborhood pest's longing pleas of "When can I ride it?" were answered (in condescending tones) with, "Maybe some day—if you can kick-start it."

Though Harley reprised the bar-and-shield tank emblems first seen for 1963, the company gave the Electra Glide new paneling to give it a unique look. This FLH was restored by Elmer Ehnes.

How do I know? That's the answer I got. And I can tell you that it sure looked like a man-sized job to me then. Now, many years later, it doesn't seem like such a big deal, but unless you're impelled by a very strong desire to take a Knucklehead or Duo-Glide for a ride, kick-starting the beast seems like more trouble than it is worth.

Here's the drill: Choke on one or two clicks. Retard the spark. Open the throttle all the way. Leap up and give a priming kick, and then another. Turn on the ignition. Push slowly down on the kick starter until you feel the compression build. Gather your strength. Then leap up and come down on the lever with all the force you can muster, while still keeping your demeanor as nonchalant as possible.

If all is well, the mighty beast springs to life and you feel like a hero.

If not, you kick some more and swear to the gods of V-twin thunder that you'll give the bike a complete tune-up this Sunday—right after you go to church. And this is not something you want to

For 1965, the four-rib gear-case cover was replaced by a new, unribbed, unpolished, sand-cast cover.

go through after stalling at an intersection, with a bunch of honking cars behind you.

Die-hard traditionalists were seriously unhappy with the new Push-Button Pan. Not only had The Motor Company taken away their central initiation rite, but the starter and huge new battery added more than 75 pounds to an already portly machine. Say hello to the Hawg.

Everyone else, though, was thrilled, despite the extra weight, and sales rose by 26 percent. The new E-Glide was the biggest-selling Harley Big

Twin since 1951, when the British invasion was in full assault.

The Electra Glide was a Harley Big Twin for the motorcycling equivalent of "the masses." That is, it was not just for the young and strong. Anyone who could swing a leg over it could start and ride it. Older riders, smaller riders, and those with weak knees could join the sport and cruise America on the ultimate long-haul touring bike of the day. In one brilliant bout of refinement, Harley-Davidson had paved the next stretch of Civility Road.

Models, Prices, and Option Groups

First-year Electra Glides were offered in two basic models—FL Super Solo and FLH Super Sport—and in foot-shift or hand-shift versions of each. Foot-shift machines were designated FLHFB and FLFB. The hand-shift machines were FLHB and FLB. Why the letter "B" to denote electric start? You're guess is as good as mine, but I think I know why they didn't use the letter "E," which would seem to have been the logical choice. That letter had been used to denote the Traffic Combination motors sold from 1953 to 1956, so Harley-Davidson wanted to avoid any chance of confusion. Per usual practice, neither the "B" nor the "F" was stamped onto the case as part of the motor number. Police or sidecar gearing was also available as a no-cost option.

Adding electric start to create the Electra Glide meant very substantial updates, and all those updates carried pretty substantial prices. The FLHs retailed for $1,595, and the FLs retailed for $1,530, each a $145 increase in price over the previous year. Standard for that price were an electric starter, black front safety guard, 5.00×16-inch black wheels and tires, air cleaner, jiffy stand, and 5-gallon gas tanks (foot-shift models only; hand-shift models had the old 3¾-gallon tanks), but four solo and two police option groups were offered to dress up the

The Electra Glide was still powered by the Panhead motor, but much of the rest of the bike was new. This view shows the new, cast-aluminum primary cases that rigidly connected the motor to the transmission and provided a flex-free mount to handle the torque of the electric starter. These cases are shown in their correct, unpolished form. Also shown is the optional one-piece heel-and-toe shifter that was new for 1965. Toe shifters were standard on all foot-shift Panheads, but a separate, add-on heel shifter could be ordered on the earlier Panheads. The Electra Glide's speedometer was the same as the one that had been introduced in 1962. This bike is fitted with the optional steering damper (operated by the knob that sprouts from the handlebar cover).

For 1965 only, the rear safety guard attaches to the upper shock-mount stud. Gone are the optional chrome-plated dome caps to cover the top of the shock absorbers, replaced by the new shock caps shown here.

The extra-large 12-volt battery necessary to power the new electric starter was much too large to fit into the former location in the "U" of the oil tank, so the oil tank was redesigned. The new tank was square and mounted to the left side of the bike, with the battery to its right. To allow clearance for these components, a new frame was introduced that lacked the "step down" in front of the top shock mounts. The result was a chunkier look that really shows the weight the Panhead put on in the 18 years since it was introduced.

basic bike. The rider tool kit was no longer included but could be ordered separately.

The Chrome Finish Group F-1 was a way to really dress up one's Electra Glide with most of the polished and chromed accessories anyone could want, all for one package price. It included the following items:

- chrome clutch-booster-spring cover, exhaust-pipe covers, front safety guard, instrument panel, mirror, oil-tank strip, muffler, rims, shock-absorber covers, spark-coil cover, and timer cover
- rubber-mounted chrome handlebars (choice of speedster or buckhorn)
- rear-chain oiler
- oil filter (attached)
- polished brake side cover, fork sliders, handlebar cover, and headlamp nacelle
- stainless steel fork covers

The King of the Highway Group contained even more dress-up accessories and had to be ordered with the Chrome Finish Group. It included:

- chrome axle and fork-stud cover (attached), battery cover, boot guard, front and rear bumpers, rear-fender tip, luggage carrier, rear safety guard, and oil tank
- extra-quiet chrome dual mufflers
- compensating sprocket
- front hub cap (attached)

- directional signals
- white fiberglass saddlebags
- solo windshield (choice of blue, clear, or red)
- super deluxe buddy seat (choice of red and white, black and white, or all white).

Optional for all King of the Highway Groups: "Normal-tone" dual mufflers could be substituted for the super-quiet mufflers, and black fiberglass saddlebags and carrier could be substituted for white at no extra charge.

King of the Highway Group F-6 was the same as F-5 except that the frame-mounted buddy seat replaced the super deluxe buddy seat.

King of the Highway Group F-7 was the deluxe touring package for solo riders, substituting the deluxe solo seat for the super deluxe buddy seat.

Standard Police Group FP-1 included:

- deluxe solo seat
- foot-controlled rear-wheel siren
- rear-chain oiler
- oil filter
- clear solo windshield
- special police speedometer
- speedometer hand control.

Police Group FP-2 was the same as FP-1 but also included a hand control for the siren.

Factory Paint Options

The two-tone paint scheme on the tank was changed once again for 1965. Instead of broad white tank panels of 1964, the 1965 tanks had white bottom panels with a pinstripe along the panel edge. Fenders were painted in the tank color, without panels.

Two standard color combinations were offered: Holiday Red with white tank bottoms and Black with white tank bottoms. Optional were Hi-Fi Blue with White tank bottoms, Hi-Fi Red with White tank bottoms, Police Silver (Police Group only), and Birch White (Police Group only). The bar-and-shield emblem was used on the tanks again for 1965.

The two-tone paint scheme on the tank was changed once again for 1964. Instead of racing stripes, the 1964 tanks had broad white side panels. The Panheads were offered in two standard color combinations: Fiesta Red with white tank panels and Black with white tank stripes. Optional were Hi-Fi Blue with white tank stripes, Hi-Fi Red with white tank panels, Police Silver (Police Group only), and Birch White (Police Group only).

Chassis Updates & Detail Changes

Turning the Duo-Glide into the Electra Glide was largely a matter of modifying the engine for the electric starter, but to get all that, the chassis required a number of changes, too.

Fully outfitted for touring, the Electra Glide was the longest, tallest, widest, and most massive touring machine of its day. This unrestored full-dress 1965 FLH was painted in the standard Holiday Red and white paint scheme.

The Electra Glide's oil tank was black, but an optional chrome strip was available to dress it up. If the bike is an FLH, the new-style FLH decal shown in the photo was attached to the chrome strip.

Chrome-plated fishtail mufflers were the standard mufflers on dual-exhaust systems, and these mufflers were offered in regular and super-quiet versions. Chrome-plated "straight-type" mufflers were optional on dual systems.

Oil Tank, Filter, and Lines

The most noticeable of these changes was to the under-seat area, where the battery and oil tank reside. With the electric starter came the need for a large battery. The 32-amp, 12-volt battery needed to reliably crank the 1200-cc Panhead motor was far too large to fit in the traditional battery recess at the rear of the U-shaped oil tank.

As large as the Panhead's frame was, there was no other place left that was big enough for such a battery, so the oil tank received its first drastic redesign in nearly three decades. Gone was the lovely horseshoe-shaped tank that had been such a big part of the Harley look since 1936, replaced by a squat, rectangular tank offset to the left side so the battery could sit on the right. Also gone were the metal oil lines and chromed filter, replaced by rubber lines and a filter that fit inside the filler hole of the oil tank.

The new tank and battery box were a step forward in function, but many think they were a step backward in style. Where the horseshoe oil tank had given the earlier Big Twins a wasp-waisted look, the Electra Glide's blocky battery and oil tank were prominent love handles, contributing more than any other feature to the impression that the Big Twin had truly reached middle age and was losing the battle of the bulge.

Given the Harley mindset, however, that bulge became another place to hang more chrome. If the Chrome Finish Group was ordered, a special chrome strip was attached to the oil tank. On FLH models, a new-style FLH decal consisting of an H and a checkered flag on a rectangular background was affixed to the left side of the tank. The King of the Highway Group included a chrome cover to at least put the battery out of sight.

Frame

To accommodate the new battery and oil tank, the frame was redesigned. It was still a straight-leg, swing-arm frame with a steering-head lock, but it no longer had the "step down" from the shock-mount forgings to the upper frame rails. This accentuated the look of greater mass in the midsection.

"Interstate" Gas Tanks

Contributing even more to the "wide-load" look of the Electra Glide were the new, 5-gallon "Interstate" gas tanks fitted to the foot-shift Electra Glides. These tanks were shaped much like the 3 ¾-gallon tanks used on the Duo-Glides but were substantially wider. The bar-and-shield emblem was used on the tanks again for 1965.

Hand-shift Electra Glides were fitted with the old 3 ¾-gallon tanks, according to the order blanks. The 3 ¼-gallon tanks were also available on special order for foot-shift bikes.

The Electra Glide used the "tombstone" speedometer that had first been used in 1962, and the speedometer was housed in the same instrument cover (fitted with the green neutral indicator light) that had been fitted to foot-shift Panheads since 1962. This speedometer and cover were both passed on to the new Shovelhead Electra Glides for 1966 and 1967.

Front End

Largely, the Electra Glide inherited the front end of the last Duo-Glides. One noticeable difference, though: the fender proudly carried a chromed "Electra Glide" emblem (no hyphen used on the emblem, though one often was in the Harley literature of the time), on each side, starting a tradition that would endure for more than 30 years.

The forks were the same as those of 1964, except that new fork top brackets were fitted to both the adjustable and non-adjustable forks. Trim and headlight nacelle were unchanged, but, of course, a 12-volt sealed-beam headlight was fitted.

Handlebars

Two-piece handlebars were fitted to the new E-Glide, as they had been to Duo-Glides since 1960, but left and right bars were slightly revised. The left bar no longer was fitted with a control spiral (because the timer is now automatically advanced), and the right bar was fitted with a starter button.

These bars were still available in Speedster or Buckhorn style for no extra charge and could also be ordered in rubber-mounted form. Rubber-mounted bars were chrome-plated; solid-mounted bars were painted black.

Horn

Sadly, the Jubilee horn died with the Duo-Glide. It was replaced by a smaller, 12-volt horn that

mounted in the same position on the left side of the engine as the body for the Jubilee horn had, but the new horn lacked the long, graceful trumpet that crossed through the V of the cylinders and curved forward on the right side.

Rear Fender

The rear fender was also revised to accommodate the new, non-step-down" frame. Like the Duo-Glide fender it replaced, the new fender had front and rear halves that joined together at a hinge so the rear half may be swung upwards for easier tire changes.

Rear Crashbars and Shocks

First-year Electra Glides were fitted with unique rear crashbars. The top mount of each no longer fastened to the frame in front of the top shock mount. Instead, the guard seemed to sprout from the center of the top shock mount. To allow this

Top: Also new for 1965 were the hand-lever assemblies, with cast-aluminum levers and mounts and ball ends on the levers. The new black push button on the right bar is the starter button.

Above: Electra Glide also wore the same dash that had been introduced in 1962.

The ElectraGlide inherited the front end of the last Duo-Glide, but a few changes were made. Handlebars were revised to delete the control spiral from the left bar, which had been used to advance or retard the spark. That spiral wasn't needed on the ElectraGlide because the new bike was fitted with automatic advance.

"sprouting," the domed shock-absorber caps of the Duo-Glide were replaced by new chromed caps that encircled the shock-absorber stud.

Rear safety guards were included in the King of the Highway package, but could also be ordered separately, painted black or chrome plated.

Besides the new caps, the only change to the shock absorbers was to the adjusting ring at the bottom of the shock, which had 12 holes (previous shocks had only 4).

Rear-Chain Guards

Two rear-chain guards were available on the Electra Glide. Standard was the valanced rear guard that had been introduced in 1963. This gloss-black-painted guard covered the top length of drive chain and the top of the rear sprocket.

Optional was a two-piece chromed chain enclosure that covered the upper and lower lengths of chain and wrapped all the way around the back of the rear sprocket. This rear-chain guard had been introduced about midway through the 1964 model year.

Motor Updates

Of course, most of the engine updates resulted from the changes to electric start and the 12-volt charging system. Nevertheless, Harley's designers made many other changes.

Electric Start

From the left, massive, new primary covers were the most apparent change. The solenoid for the starter jutted forward from the clutch bulge of the inner cover, and the electric starter attached to the motor side of the inner cover just above the clutch assembly, lying transversely across between the transmission and oil tank. These new primary covers were the backbone of the new electric-start system.

Stamped-steel inner primary covers used on the Hydra-Glides and Duo-Glides attached only to the engine but not to the transmission and were far too flimsy to hold a high-torque starter motor in precise alignment with the starter gear on the clutch. The solution was to design new inner and outer primary covers that would rigidly link the motor and transmission and would provide a rigid mount for the new starter. Harley cast these new covers from aluminum.

Rigid they were, but one result was that the transmission could no longer be moved in its mounts to adjust the primary chain, so an adjustable chain tensioner was mounted to the inner primary cover. Access to this tensioner was provided by a removable plate in the center of the outer cover. This plate was shaped like an elongated oval and attached to the cover with four screws. It is to this plate that the new-style buddy-seat foot pegs attached. Both inner and outer primary covers were unpolished and unpainted.

Also inside the primary covers was a new clutch assembly. This new clutch used the same plates and springs as the 1964 clutch, but almost everything else was new, including the clutch hub, clutch pushrod, main-shaft nut, clutch rod, and clutch release lever. Most important, the clutch shell was fitted with a ring gear to mate with the starter-shaft gear that was driven by the electric starter. On hand-shift bikes, the clutch was operated by a revised foot lever, and on foot-shift bikes, the clutch was operated by a new, die-cast aluminum hand-lever assembly.

Never a company to cut its own throat with forced change, Harley-Davidson left the kick starter in place on the Electra Glide. For those who refused to compromise their manliness, H-D made special plates to cover the starter and solenoid holes after the contemptible new devices were removed. It was also possible that new machines could be special ordered from the factory without the electric starter.

Automatic Advance
Inside the Electra Glide beat the heart of the Duo-Glide, with a new, automatic-advance pacemaker that worked with its electric starter to make the whole bike more user friendly. No longer was a complicated CPR ritual required to restart that heart. No more manually retarding the timing and kicking over the motor two or three times with the ignition off to prime the motor. All that was necessary on the E Glide was a notch or two of choke and a gentle touch to the starter button. Then, when it was time to ride off, no more worrying about advancing the timing.

Crankcases
The motor itself was largely unchanged from the outside-oiler motor that had first been introduced in 1963, but it was given new cases and was connected rigidly to the transmission by the radically new primary-chain housing described earlier.

The left crankcase was redesigned to bolt up to the new inner primary cover, and the right case was redesigned to eliminate the boss on which the

spark-control cable mounted (this boss originally held the generator cut-out relay). Also, the breather tube no longer extended through a tunnel in both cases to the primary-chain housing. Instead, the breather pipe extended across behind the case. The primary chain is now lubricated by oil routed to the chain case from the redesigned oil pump.

"Smooth" Gear Cover
On the right, the most visible change was the new, smooth gear cover. Like the cover used in 1963–1964, the new cover had oil passages to feed the oil lines to the heads, but the new cover lacked the four horizontal cooling fins. Instead, the cover was flat, with a fairly rough, sand-cast texture. The factory supplied this cover in unpolished form. It was secured with straight-slot screws.

A chrome hubcap was included in the King of the Highway package, or could be ordered separately. The removable cover in the hubcap gave access to the wheel hub's grease fitting.

Touring packages for the Electra Glide included the same fiberglass bags that had been introduced for 1963.

Inside the light housings were 12-volt bulbs to accommodate the higher voltage that came with the electric start.

Electra Glides were available with sprung or frame-mounted buddy seats. Shown here is the red-and-white sprung buddy seat.

12-Volt Electrics

In the early 1960s, automobile and motorcycle manufacturers began switching from 6-volt to 12-volt electrical systems. Harley-Davidson followed suit on its Servi-Cars for 1964 and on the Electra Glide for 1965 because 12-volt systems have overwhelming advantages over 6-volt systems for motorcycle use.

What are they? Since the 12-volt system operates at twice the voltage, the generator needs to supply only half the amperage to generate the same amount of power. And because the components have to carry only half the amperage, all components in the system—generator, starter, wire gauge, and others—can be made much smaller and lighter. A by-product of the reduction in wire gauge is that more loops of wire can then be wrapped around the armature and field coils of the generator, resulting in greater current output than would be possible in a 6-volt generator of the same size.

The new 12-volt generator was a two-brush design that made use of a separate voltage regulator. It was mounted across the front of the motor and was driven by a gear in the gear case, just like the 6-volt generator it replaced, and was attached by hex-head screws. The new generator put out enough power that it was also used on radio-equipped police bikes.

To accommodate the Electra Glide's new electrical system, 12-volt bulbs were used in the headlight, taillight, and in the optional spotlights, parking lights, and turn signals.

Exhaust Pipes and Mufflers

Electra Glides came standard with a single exhaust much like those of the last Duo-Glides. Header pipes of the new system were identical to the old except that each header pipe of the new system fastened to its cylinder-head exhaust nipple using a new-for-1965 ferrule-style clamp made of stainless steel. Optional chrome header-pipe covers were still available, as was a chrome-plated, clamp-on pipe guard for the front header. The S-pipe and Y-pipe were new for 1965, and on some later Electra Glides, the two pipes were combined into an elongated Y-pipe. These pipes were chrome plated. The standard muffler was the same style of black-painted tubular muffler that had first been introduced in 1950 as the Mellow-Tone muffler and updated in 1952 as the Low-Tone muffler. A chrome-plated muffler was optional, as was the "finned and extension" chrome fishtail muffler.

Three optional dual exhausts could be ordered, differing only in the choice of mufflers. Available were dual exhausts with the chromed short "straight-type" (short versions of the Low-Tone muffler that had been introduced in 1958), normal-tone fishtail mufflers, and the extra-quiet fishtail mufflers.

Electra Glide Production

The motorcycle market was on the rise during 1965, and Harley-Davidson sales rose along with all other manufacturers'. Electra Glide sales were 2,130 FLB and 4,800 FLHB, for a total of 6,930 Electra Glides (about 26 percent higher than sales of the 1964 Duo-Glide). For perspective, this is the highest sales year for Harley's Big Twin since 1951.

Requiem Panhead

During the 18 years the Panhead was in production, the whole American motorcycle business was transformed. When the Panhead made its debut in 1948, Harley-Davidson was the world's largest motorcycle company and Indian was still a viable concern, but the British motorcycle manufacturers were coming on strong and a man named Soichiro had just founded Honda Motors. By 1965, Harley-Davidson was the only American motorcycle manufacturer left, the British bike craze was already on the wane, and Honda alone was selling more motorcycles in the United States than all other manufacturers combined.

And the Panhead was itself transformed in many ways. The first Panheads were trim and elemental large-bore sporting machines that even with saddlebags and a windshield were still relatively light at under 600 pounds. By 1958, the

Optional fender tips and bumpers for front and rear were the same as those used on the late Duo-Glides.

Left: That ribbed chrome cover hides the massive 12-volt battery added to operate the electric start.

Below: Electra Glide was fitted with new, larger, 5-gallon gas tanks. These tanks gave the machine a muscular look and gave America's new ultra-tourer a range of 200–250 miles.

Electric start and automatic advance made the Electra Glide as easy to start as a Honda 50. Strong legs and an arcane starting ritual were no longer required.

Below: The optional windshield was available with clear, blue, or red lower panels.

Right: The cap and oil lines to the new oil tank were underneath the seat. Instead of the metal lines used with the old oil tank, rubber lines were used for the oil and breather lines to the new oil tank. Just below the filler cap is the new, internal oil filter that was optional for 1965. The old-style external oil filter was no longer used.

Panhead had suspension at both ends but weighed closer to 700 pounds and gave away all sporting pretense to its smaller brother, the Sportster. By 1965, the Panhead Electra Glide was a behemoth, a two-wheeled land yacht that weighed more than 700 pounds in stripped form, but started at the touch of a button. Add fiberglass saddlebags, a windshield, dual exhaust, chrome bits, and a cigarette lighter, and the Electra Glide could top 800 pounds. The classic American touring bike was born.

For 1966, Harley's Big Twin motor was given yet another top end, and a new Harley moniker was coined: the Shovelhead, which stayed in production for 19 years. The Shovelhead-powered Electra Glide would go through its own evolution, getting disc brakes, alternating-current electrics, and a full fairing. Before long, the Electra Glide would also devolve into more elemental machines such as the Super Glide, Low Rider, and eventually the sporting FXRS, a bike that helped Harley-Davidson through some tough times.

In the early 1980s, the trend toward a kinder, gentler Big Twin that started with the first Panhead in 1948 resulted in the Evolution Big Twins that put Harley-Davidson back on the road to prosperity.

As this is written in the spring of 2002, Harley-Davidson is about to introduce its 100th Anniversary line. Among the best sellers will likely be the Softail and Road King models that carry forward into Harley's second century the classic styles set on the Panhead springers, Hydra-Glides, and Duo-Glides. There could be no more meaningful testament to their timeless appeal.

Index